G000115863

The *Path* *That* Beckons

Taking the Next Step on the Journey
to a Life You Love

Debbie Lamb Turner

The Path That Beckons
Taking the Next Step on the Journey to a Life You Love

Copyright © 2015 Debbie Lamb Turner

Published by:
Transformation Books
211 Pauline Drive #513
York, PA 17402
www.TransformationBooks.com

ISBN: 9780996827133
Library of Congress Control No: 2016930298

Cover design by: Skip Nall, *www.skipnallphoto.com*
Layout and typesetting: Ranilo Cabo
Editor: Marlene Oulton
Proofreader: Michelle Cohen
Book Midwife: Carrie Jareed

Printed in the United States of America

The *Path* That *Beckons*

Taking the Next Step on the Journey
to a Life You Love

The following pages are written in honor of that warm loving Light that illuminates our path and reminds us, even in our darkest valleys, that we are never alone.

Acknowledgements

To adequately thank the many people who have contributed to my life and brought me to this place in time would take an entire book of its own. The people mentioned here are few; I hold the rest of you, along with all the lessons you've provided, close to my heart. Thank you.

To my husband and best friend, Mike, for his sweet love, relentless belief in me, and telling me the truth, even when I don't really want to hear it. There is no one I'd rather be walking hand in hand with on this crazy awesome journey of life. My most valuable treasures, my children and the special ones they've chosen to share their journeys with; Stacey, Mike, Jake, Amy, Jeff, and Jenny for their support even though I'm sure they question my sanity most days; my precious grandchildren for reminding me of the pure beauty and goodness in the world; my sweet brother, Tony, who gave me one of the best compliments ever, "You've got balls"; my sisters and cohorts Sylvia and Katy, for always being in my corner. Having the love and cheering section of my family as I've walked this path has meant everything to me. I love you.

To the many 'Sistahs' who I've shared Sisters on Purpose retreats, weekend getaways, coffee and cake get-togethers with: you are my inspiration. Thank you for allowing me to learn from you as you authentically and unselfishly share your trials and triumphs in an effort to encourage, empower and lift up other women. I am proud to be your sister.

Since making the decision that now's the time to write, I have been encircled by an inspiring group of people who closely walked this trail with me every step of the way. Thank you to Christine Kloser for her 'Get Your Book Done' program. See, it really works! For my publishing team at Transformation Books: Carrie, who answered all my questions, calmed my concerns , and went above and beyond in so many ways; Ranilo, for designing a beautiful cover and sitting with me on Skype to tweak everything until it was 'perfect'; Allison, for revising my back cover and bringing it all together so well; and Marlene, whose sensitivity and sense of humor made the editing process fun.

My heartfelt appreciation goes out to the contributors of the stories at the end of each chapter. The genuine authentic sharing of your deeply personal experiences, some of which are being told for the first time, is inspirational beyond words. Thank you all so much. Each and every one of your stories matter, not just to me, but to all who are honored to witness them. And most importantly, YOU matter. I love you all.

As a reader, if you are inspired by or resonate with the story of any woman in particular and would like to let them know, you may contact them at *www.ThePathThatBeckons.com.* There are also links to causes or businesses they are passionate about or affiliated with so you can get involved or support them.

Table of Contents

Introduction

Growing up, I was anything but adventurous. I was a rule-following, goody-two-shoes kinda kid. My greatest act of pushing the envelope was trying a Marlboro when I was thirteen, standing alone in front of the bathroom mirror at my friend's house to see if I looked cool – which I definitely DID NOT. Staring back at me were two watery eyes and a red face encircled in smoke and a whole lot of coughing going on. At a party two weeks later, it seemed more prudent to simply hold the skinny Eve cigarette between my fingers for effect, but the coolness factor still evaded me. Thankfully, I gave up my smoking habit! Then there was the time in junior high when I ditched school with twelve of my closest friends and cousins thinking no one would notice. Obviously, I wasn't very good at rebellion.

I don't regret my youthful naiveté nor do I feel I missed out on anything. My childhood and teen years were happy ones spending my free time participating in drill team, pep club, drama, and church activities. The small town I grew up in valued marriage and family, so not surprisingly, my desire to please and "do the right thing," played a big part in my decision to marry my long-time high school boyfriend one week after I graduated. I became a mom and had three children by the time I was 24. I embraced that calling and give thanks every day for the amazing children I am blessed with in my life.

Yet something BIG shifted within me as I approached my 40th birthday.

My children, ages 16, 18, and 20, no longer required as much of my time and energy as they were starting to make their way out into the world to follow their own dreams. I was forced to face the uncomfortable realization that I could no longer busy myself with the daily needs of my family, but instead must take an honest look at my life and marriage. Like many couples, my husband and I had morphed from being partners into just being parents. It became increasingly easier to avoid dealing with our relationship that was slipping away than to expend the effort it would take restoring and revitalizing that union. You always think you can work on things later, but sometimes a day arrives when you realize it's too late. It's a classic story you've heard time and again of how people simply grow apart over time. However, when it's happening to you, you feel like you're the only one; and the feelings of sadness and failure are overwhelming.

With the big 4-0 just around the corner, I took a fresh look at myself. It became crystal clear that I had lived my entire life trying to please everyone else and to be what I thought was expected of me; an obedient daughter, a supportive wife, polite, hardworking, considerate, and the list goes on. I don't blame anyone else for these expectations as I placed them on myself in an effort to be recognized as "good enough." But now it was time to grow up. I was turning forty freaking years old! Time to make my own choices, discover who I really am, and live my truth – unapologetically.

I made a bold announcement. I would be spending my upcoming birthday in Cabo San Lucas, Mexico. I would go for two days alone and then anyone that wanted could join me for the next two days. I desperately needed a couple days to wrap my head around this new awareness that I was responsible for my own life, and explore how to move forward into the second half of it.

This was the most adventurous move I had ever made in my life for many reasons. I had never been on a trip of this magnitude alone. I had never even been out of the country. I didn't speak or understand a word of Spanish. And, I didn't ask anyone's opinion or permission. It was unrealistic and unreasonable… and yet I did it.

During my time alone, I searched my soul asking tough questions. "Who am I, really? If I set aside making others happy, how do I really want to live my life? How can I be the best version of myself? What are my true talents and gifts, and how can I share them with others?" And then the big one: "So, what do I do now?"

I learned a lot about myself that weekend. I discovered a passion for travel and exploring new areas. I found I wasn't nearly as scared or timid as I'd been pretending to be all my life. I reconnected with my love of writing. I began to see my potential as an encourager of others. I unearthed a deeper level of spirituality as I placed my sincere requests for clarity and direction in the hands of my Heavenly Father. I found strength and courage buried deep in my core I wasn't aware I possessed. I remembered who I was created to be.

I came back home with the resolve to live a life true to myself. This realization made complete sense in my head, and my heart agreed it was the right thing; but moving forward to execute the plan was still gut-wrenching. I didn't want to achieve my own dreams at the expense of those I loved most in my life, and my first decision did cause pain. I like to think I handled it in the most caring and sensitive way possible, but I don't think it's ever painless or easy for a child to hear their parents are divorcing.

Yes, this was definitely a turning point in my life. Many times I've felt myself standing at a crossroad where I knew my choice would have an impact on the rest of my life. I wish I could say my choices have always lead me down the "right" path with beautiful wild flowers and melodious music playing in the background, but that's not so. I've gone down trails I've regretted and have had to continuously keep choosing a new route, but that's part of life. I'm so grateful for finding the courage to go down that first path where I embarked on my personal journey of self-discovery, self-expression, and authenticity.

What moments in your life have called you to step out onto a new path? Is there a situation or occurrence that caused, or forced, you to see yourself or your existence in a new way? One that has inspired you to be called to do or be something more?

Maybe you're feeling it right now. You feel that nudge or yearning, but you're not even sure what it means. Are you willing to explore the next path that is beckoning and where it will lead? There are many paths – neither right nor wrong – that take you a little farther down the road of your life's journey. And believe me, some are more gentle than others.

I've meandered down the path of healing, the path of spirituality, and the path of gratitude. Some paths I go down many times, each time discovering something new.

In the following chapters, we'll explore various paths and why that choice may be appropriate for you. I invite you to take your time as you go through this book. The questions are posed to help you inquire and dig a little deeper into your beliefs, what may be holding you back, and ways to move forward. Some questions will take time and energy to explore fully. My hope is you are inspired or receive clarity about which path might beckon you to take that first step with ease and grace.

Time to Fly

The back side of my home is almost entirely windows. Every room offers lovely views of the backyard with its lush green grass, mesquite trees, colorful geraniums, pansies, and miscellaneous foliage. The windows illuminate the interior of the house and invite in the outdoors. Maybe a little too well.

On any given day, if you look closely, there's a good chance you'll see the imprint of a dove in flight on one of the windows. Occasionally, a feather is still stuck to the glass as a sad reminder of the mishap.

Many unsuspecting birds come to an abrupt halt as they collide with these invisible barriers. I've actually witnessed this unfortunate encounter a time or two. It's typically the same scenario. The bird smacks into the glass, then it's knocked back and down onto the patio. It sits there stunned for a few seconds, shakes its head a bit, and eventually resumes flight – this time *away from* the window!

Have you ever felt like this bird? Just flying along the familiar routine of your life when suddenly you're whacked upside the head by something completely unexpected? It may show up in the form of a suspicious mammogram, loss of a job, or a driver who didn't see you stopped at the traffic light in front of him until it was too late.

Maybe you've had your world shaken by a miscarriage, infidelity, divorce, or loss of a loved one. If so, where are you in the recovery process?

Are you still sitting shocked and shaken? Have you moved into feeling the pain and are now grieving? Or are you focused on getting grounded and centered again?

Wherever you are in the process is okay. Just do a quick check-in with yourself to identify that place, and recognize you don't have to stay stuck in any of those steps forever.

There is a path beckoning you right now. You're being called to something even as you read these words. All that's required of you is to be willing to hear that call and take the first step on a journey to a joyful, fulfilling, and amazing life you love.

It's time to fly.

Part 1

Clearing the Path

Chapter 1

The Path of Gratitude

"If the only prayer you said in your whole life was,
thank you, that would suffice."
– Meister Eckhart

I've been called a Pollyanna a time or two. I guess that's because I choose to anticipate the rainbow during the thunderstorm and expect the proverbial light at the end of the tunnel.

As a child, I was encouraged to get my head out of the clouds because I spent a lot of time daydreaming instead of dealing with what others saw as the "real world." But, that real world seemed like other people's reality, not mine. My "real world" was a much more pleasant place. I'm sure there have been several people concerned for my well-being and believed I was in for a rude awakening when I realized just how harsh and cruel life really was.

People are sometimes uncomfortable around dreamers or optimists, which I believe is because they don't clearly understand the rationale behind that mode of thinking. When I say I'm optimistic, I don't mean stupid, as there's a world of difference between those two states of being. I don't say, "Hey, let's jump off that bridge. It'll be okay." (Remember, I told you in the Introduction I'm not a rule breaker.) I don't bury my head in the sand ignoring what is, but I recognize the positive aspects of situations, expecting good outcomes. At the same time, I'm aware when things aren't perfect and when there's room for improvement. I just choose not to dwell in the negativity. In the end, when it comes down to it, I'll always choose that half-full glass over that half-empty one. And, even if it is empty, I know it can be refilled.

I find it both comical and ironic that I ended up in the insurance industry through my search for a career to help support my family. I remember many times sitting across the desk with my clients reviewing perils to insure against and thinking to myself, "That won't ever happen." However, I kept those opinions to myself as my job was to help protect them against anything that *could* happen, not to share my eternal optimism.

So where do you stand on the half-empty/half-full dilemma? Do you vacillate back and forth at any given moment? Most people do, so don't think you're in the "wrong" cheerleading section for believing in both ideas.

Just for the record, let me be clear that I am not always positive. I have my moments of negativity and feeling sorry for myself, just like everyone else. I simply try to minimize how long I allow myself to wallow before I return to reality. (Okay, yes, MY reality.) I'm not a positive person because I lead a charmed life or I haven't had my share of trials. I simply choose to live in a positive state... most of the time.

To put things into perspective, my parents were divorced when I was two years old and I grew up in a blended family. My mother was diagnosed with type 1 diabetes when she was 29, and after two heart attacks and then bypass surgery at the age of 46, she passed away at the young age of 59. My birth father, whom I consider myself close to even though I didn't live with him, also passed when he was just 59. I've had three miscarriages, gone through bankruptcy, and been divorced. As an adult, after my children were grown and on their own and I remarried, my home burned to the ground, destroying everything my husband and I owned except the clothes on our back. I contracted a lung disorder where I nearly died. I found myself dependent on oxygen for several months to stay alive and was hospitalized three times. I've had a concussion (which happened while visiting a foreign country), a broken foot, a broken ankle, a fractured heel and broken arm, a benign lump removed from my neck, and a cancerous melanoma taken off my back. At one point, doctors suspected I had lymphoma (which, thankfully, was not the case), and in the process of taking a biopsy which revealed I had valley fever, one of my vocal cords was damaged. I was left without the use of my voice for two months. As I said, I've had my trials just like everyone else.

My secret to positivity and remaining optimistic in the face of whatever I am up against is extremely simple – gratitude.

So, let's wander down the *Path of Gratitude* together, shall we?

If looking on the bright side of things and being grateful sounds a little too easy or too good to be true, let me say this: it is, but not always, and definitely not at first. It takes a little training and reprograming to think differently. It is easier to be negative and complain rather than feel grateful and appreciative. Think about it. When you're talking with someone, how often is negativity part of the conversation? All the time! Comments like "This traffic is ridiculous! Why don't they get another checker? That's just the way life is!" pepper our everyday language. Whole genres of music are based on telling stories of how bad things are in the world. We've gotten so good at complaining, we don't even recognize it most times.

Isn't that sad? Look around you. Right now. Chances are you're sitting in a warm, comfortable place, protected from the elements, or better yet, outside enjoying a beautiful day. You have clothes on your body, probably a full stomach, or at least you don't have to worry if you'll have a next meal. You are educated and can read. You live at a time when you can communicate and stay in contact with someone around the world by picking up a telephone or through many forms of social media. You are free to leave your home when you feel like it, talk to who you want, and travel where you want. Life is pretty awesome!

It's a choice. You can dwell on the events or circumstances that you deem as "bad" or you can look at the millions of ways your existence is amazing. It's all a choice.

Life can be hard, I admit that. We experience situations that rock us to our core. There are events that blindside us, and some we couldn't begin to prepare for even if we had time. I don't minimize those times. Illness, loss of a loved one, heartbreak... those, and many others, are very real and hurt beyond what words can describe. In these moments of extreme pain, I don't advocate you pretend they aren't happening and ignore their existence. My suggestion is to allow yourself to feel them fully. Experience what you need to for the amount of time you need to process them. Then pick yourself up when the time is right, and move on. Don't let an event shape who you are, paralyze your growth, and cause you to have a hard, resentful heart. None of those serve you.

As you're reading this chapter, if something comes to mind that is painful and negatively affecting your life past the time you believe it should, make a note of it. In the next chapter, *The Path of Healing*, you'll have an opportunity to work through those hurts which is essential for your well-being.

I find it's usually not the major catastrophes that keep me in a dark or negative place, it's those little every day annoyances. My car won't start, someone cuts me off in traffic, I misplace my keys, things like that. (I just realized my examples are all driving related. Do you think I have issues?) It's the little things that stick in your craw and keep you cranky.

So, how do you deal with those annoyances?

There are several gratitude practices you can implement into your daily routine to help keep you in a positive place and allow more good to enter your life.

One of my favorite practices is journaling. Let me say right now, I love journaling. It's my passion, so you're likely to hear this come up again as you read on. Journaling is the method I use to ground myself and prepare my heart and my attitude for the day. Your method may be playing music, meditating, or taking a walk. Whatever approach you choose, it's important to have a practice that helps you start the day on a positive note and in a grateful frame of mind.

Almost every morning, I write. I have different purposes for writing, but whenever I'm finished with that particular purpose, I write at least one page I call my "Gratitude Page." I jot down all the things I'm thankful for in that moment. Once you start this process, the floodgates to love and abundance open. You think of something else to be grateful for, and then something else pops into your mind. The more you write, the more blessed you feel. Writing is incredibly powerful. I encourage you to try it tomorrow morning.

If you want to mix it up a bit, select a different area of your life each day and find as many things about that particular aspect where you can express gratitude. Monday – your health, Tuesday – the people in your life, Wednesday – your job, and so on. Have fun with it!

I also have a little game I play when I'm in the middle of a situation I don't consider positive or happy. I ask myself, "What's one good thing about this?" I follow up that question with, "Where is God in this equation?" These two queries help me see a positive aspect I hadn't noticed which can completely shift my perspective. Typically events aren't *good* or *bad.* Those labels are merely slapped on as a result of the meaning we've assigned to the situation at hand.

Have you ever overheard two people talking about another person? The first comments, "Susan's so nice and friendly. I really like her." The other person, in disbelief, asks, "Susan? Oh, I don't like her at all. I think she's full of herself." How does that happen? How can two people view the same person so differently? Both people are looking through their unique personal filters and perspective, each believing their opinion is the correct one.

If we can form completely different beliefs about something or someone we accept as true, how much easier would it be to form the belief that life is great; people are good; there is enough; and prosperity abounds? I just went too far, didn't I? Most people can hold a little more good in their thinking and their hearts, but not a lot all at once. So ease into it. Give gratitude and thanks a little at a time, increasing and expanding as you feel comfortable. Be sincere about it. Don't just rattle off things you think you "should" be grateful for. In what ways are you *truly* blessed?

People won't think you've lost your mind by thinking life is great. Okay, they might at first. The positive attitude you project *will* be felt by those around you. It might even catch on. Before you know it, you may hear one of your most cynical friends agreeing with your cheery comment.

The Gratitude Path is truly a magical path – one that opens your eyes to more good than you can imagine. Spend a little time here. Enjoy yourself. Allow your thinking to be transformed.

🐾 *Today's Step* 🐾

This morning, step out the door of your home (front or back, it's up to you) and look around. Open your heart and call upon all your senses. Experience everything as if it is the first time you've stood in this spot. What do you observe?

Silently, list at least ten things you see, hear, smell, or feel right now that you're grateful for and why. How do these newfound treasures bless your life? If ten comes quickly, do twenty! Isn't life magical?

East Sheen
cemetery 6/11/17

Becky Shares Her Story

"Cancer comes in all forms and in different stages. The cancer I was diagnosed with was invasive ductile breast cancer at stage 3.

Who's to say why a person gets the type and stage that they do? Did I receive this because it was over my heart and I've never felt loved in my entire life? And the heaviness of not being loved came out in this cruel manner? Or was it because I asked the Universe for new boobs and just didn't specify the method of how to get them?

Even though not everything always went right in my life, I did have a lot to be grateful for. I have my beautiful daughter, my friends, not much debt, a place to live, and money to enjoy life with. Even in the beginning of all this, I started a journal and acknowledged how grateful I was.

However, I went through three rounds of chemotherapy and the side effects were unbearable. Thinking that I could "call the shots" I quit chemo and wanted to do surgery. But, I had a doctor who was less than understanding and yelled at me. I had to find a whole new team of doctors. And then still three more rounds were needed.

I think, no, I know, this hit me as hard as when I received the initial diagnosis. I started chemo again and received the same side effects. I went into the doctor's office a week later for my follow-up appointment. My blood count was 125, which is extremely low. With all I was going through, I still tried to be a positive person. But getting these same side effects again, I felt my negativity creeping back in.

After the doctor's visit, I went to the bookstore. I asked the Universe for help. I needed "something" to get me through this. In the self-help section was a book prominently displayed, "The Magic" by Rhonda Byrne. The title intrigued me, considering the location. Then I read the information on the back cover. The book was based on gratitude – 28 Days of Gratitude, to be exact. Maybe I'm not as grateful as I thought. Or is there a special "way" to be grateful?

I began immediately on a newer path of gratitude by following the assignments and guidelines outlined in the book.

Fourteen days later, another round of chemo was due. The doctor runs blood tests prior to each chemo to make sure the body can handle it. My blood test came back at 525! Not great, but so much letter than two short weeks ago.

While reading the book, one of the things the author recommended is to be grateful for everything that enters your body. I would receive six bags of chemo each round. As each bag was going into the IV, I would say, "Thank you for what is about to enter my body. I know it is going to heal me."

Drum roll please . . . No adverse reactions occurred from the chemo treatment! And this was only fourteen days of applying what I had read into my life.

It was 620 days from my initial diagnosis, through chemo, surgery, and radiation to receive a report that no cancer was found. And for those 620 days, I am truly grateful. Cancer was a gift given to me to change who I am and remind me how much more I need to appreciate life.

After the 28 days, I decided to continue with the journaling and to write ten things I'm grateful for every day. It is amazing the things I continue to be blessed with, and how the Universe aligns things so I have a pretty smooth road.

My path of gratitude continues daily."

If you'd like to comment or share your own story with Becky, please visit *www.ThePathThatBeckons.com.*

Focus on the shame
not unforgiven

↑

under the need to
forgive is
the need to release
the shame

Chapter 2

The Path of Healing

*"The truth is, unless you let go, unless you forgive yourself,
unless you forgive the situation, unless you realize that the
situation is over, you cannot move forward."*
– Steve Maraboli

I pride myself in being a good mother. Not perfect by any stretch of the imagination, but good. In raising my three children, I provided for their needs, kept them safe, and encouraged them to be self-sufficient in the world and decent human beings.

However, something came to light recently that had me questioning my parenting skills.

I read a short story someone wrote about their grandmother's apron. It instantly brought back an image of my Grandma Hayes, my maternal grandmother, who almost always wore an apron over her clothes around the house. I smiled as I recalled her dancing around the kitchen while making dinner with the likes of Hank Williams or Ferron Young blaring on her old hi-fi record player. She was carefree, full of life, and a fun grandma. Years after my grandpa's death and before I was in my teens, she remarried and moved to Washington state, but I have sweet memories of the two of us in my younger years. I felt special just being in her presence.

In revisiting those memories of her, I was reminded of a stark contrast to our relationship. Her interaction with my mom, her daughter, was sometimes strained. She liked to tell my mom how things should be done, even though my mom was a grown woman herself. I sense things had always been that way between then.

My mom was a lot like her own mother although I'm sure she would have argued she was nothing like her. While raising me, she was strict. I always knew my mom loved me; that was never in question. But when it came to her rules, there was no discussion. In high school, I had a curfew, and if I came in ten minutes late, my car would be taken away for a week. Period. No discussion or explanation of why I was not on time. None of that mattered. When a rule was made, that was the rule. Being the people pleaser I was, I grudgingly accepted the consequences. Looking back, I wish she had been more approachable and that I had shared my feelings, not just about the rules, but others things as well with her. I'm sure many children feel that at one time or another about their relationships with their parents.

As I became an adult, my mom showed up very differently for me in our relationship. Maybe she thought she had done her job raising me and since I turned out okay she didn't need to impart any more lessons. Maybe she felt the yearning for a deeper relationship with me, as well. Or maybe, just maybe, it was I who had changed. Whatever occurred, I'm grateful to say we had a very sweet connection as we both aged.

My daughter was my mom's first grandchild. She fell in love with Stacey instantly and was thrilled with her new title of "Grandma." The two shared a very tender relationship even though we moved six hundred miles away when Stacey was just seven years old. There was a bond between them distance couldn't sever. It's still a joke in our family that when I would hear Stacey fondly say, "Grandma said… or Grandma did…" my reply was, "I don't know who you're talking about. This is not the same woman who raised me!"

Now, let's move forward to the third chapter of this story – the one that's toughest for me to come to grips with. I look back at who I was as a mother to my precious daughter, and you guessed it. I recognize strong similarities to the previous matriarchs in my family. I made the rules. I don't regret having rules and sticking with them, but I do regret being harsh and unbendable. Stacey was (and still is) a sensitive, caring, and yes, spirited, daughter.

She lamented when she got older, "You were so much stricter with me than the boys. Your only rule by the time Jake came along was 'Don't kill anybody!'" My jokingly, half-hearted attempt at an apology was, "You were my first child. I didn't know what I was doing. Sorry." But the truth to my deep regret is that I didn't operate the same with my sons. I was more relaxed and open to conversation with them about not just the rules, but everything.

My daughter did not inherit my "people pleaser" personality. She was, and still is, I'm proud to say, a strong willed and opinionated woman. Instead of retreating to her room after a punishment she perceived as unfair, she argued her case. We butted heads a lot, neither of us willing to give in; and, many times when she was a teenager days passed without us speaking to each other. I still feel a twinge of remorse and sadness about those times as, after all, I was the adult. I was her mom, the one person who should have been always on her side regardless of the situation. Her champion. Because of the hard line I set, I know there were times she couldn't share with me difficult situations in her life and was left to navigate them alone.

Stacey now has a daughter of her own; and you know where this is going, right? She is one of the joys and lights of my life. My first grandchild AND granddaughter! It's so easy for me to love and accept her unconditionally. Many may argue this is a privilege earned as a grandparent. Parents are responsible for making sure they brush their teeth, eat good foods, act respectful, tell the truth, and the list goes on and on. As a grandparent, our job is simply to love. I agree with that philosophy, but I wish the women in my lineage had experienced more acceptance and empowerment from their moms as they were growing up.

In processing this story and recognizing how far back it goes, I recognized healing was necessary. My mother and grandmother have passed on, so there is no action to take there. I take comfort in the fact that they know I loved them and they loved me. The healing to take place now is between my daughter and me.

The two of us met for lunch recently and I recounted this story along with my sincere apology for the mistakes I made in raising her. I assured her if I had it to do all over again, I would definitely be better at it. I reminded her how very much I love her, and how proud I am of the amazing woman she is. I ended by asking her to please break this unhealthy cycle. She has a sweet little girl, ten years old now, who needs to know her mom is in her corner, cheering her on in everything she does, encouraging her uniqueness, and acknowledging who she is. The wounds were not completely healed by that one conversation; but I believe it's the first step in the healing process.

Do you harbor resentment towards someone you haven't been able to let go? Maybe that person is you. Are you haunted by guilt or shame? Has your heart been hurt to the point that you don't see how you'll be able to recover? Are you ready to heal those open wounds for good?

Those feelings, though uncomfortable, are nudging you that it's time to move forward. Before you can recognize what's calling you and raise your foot to take that first step, you may need to put a little salve on those "heart wounds" and help them heal.

Step with me onto *The Path of Healing*.

This particular path may be relatively short or it may take time and work going down. Sometimes stopping to shed light on the cause of your pain and letting it go is all that's required. Other times, the pain is deep and requires talking with a professional to help you through the process. Either way, it's worth the effort.

So, let's begin. Take a piece of paper (You didn't realize this was going to be interactive, did you?). Make a list of the first things that pop into your head with regard to the following three areas. These should be things, that when you think of them, you feel a real sting in your heart. Not like the feeling you get when someone at the grocery store pushes past you rudely, unless you have an intense feeling about that incident; rather it's things that cause you to experience a twinge of remorse when you think about them. Some areas could be:

- Resentments you hold against someone.

- Shame or guilt that you're carrying for something you haven't forgiven yourself for.

- Disappointment, regret, or deep personal sadness as a result of something said or done to you.

As you reflect over your list, are there any situations you can forgive and release immediately? Maybe it's a trivial misunderstanding with someone where you expected an apology from them, when in reality you may be at fault as well. If this is the case, do yourself a favor and make amends. I'm not suggesting you apologize for something you didn't do or take responsibility for another person's actions. I'm inviting you to consider if letting it go helps you more than holding onto whatever the slight may be.

The first step is to sit down and write ten things you love about the person you have a conflict with or ill feelings toward. Compose this list prior to the situation that's lingering, and don't include anything about that incident. Confirm who they are for you and what they bring to your life. Many times this process alone will diffuse the anger, resentment, or negative feelings you have about that person.

You then have a few choices:

- Forgive and let it go. But, you have to truly let it go. No bringing it up at a later date or using it against the person.

- Call the person and tell them what they mean to you. Apologize for your part in the misunderstanding if you choose. Depending on your relationship with the person, you will know the appropriate action.

- Write a letter to the person describing your feelings for them. (Remember, this is not a chance to bring it all up again or reiterate why you're upset.) You have the choice to mail the letter to them or to tear it up after you've finished.

The letter method is extremely helpful when the person you hold negative feelings for is no longer alive. Many people feel they've missed that opportunity and carry the unspoken pain with them for the rest of their lives. It's amazing how helpful this can be to facilitate your healing process. Writing the letter and tearing it up is also helpful when you don't want the person you feel wronged by in your life anymore, or you don't want to speak with them again. This is perfectly fine. Releasing your anger or resentment towards someone doesn't always mean you will sit down across the Thanksgiving table with them again. It simply means you let go of the hold their actions or your feelings about those actions have over you.

Penning a letter is also very helpful when the person you're angry with is yourself. Show yourself the same grace and forgiveness that you offer others. We're all just trying our best at this thing called life. We make mistakes. We fall down. We hurt other people. And we make bad choices. Those are usually not what hold us back. What keeps us stuck are the feelings we attach to those mistakes or choices. Guilt and shame are a wicked pair. Allowing them to run amok in our lives and our hearts is a recipe for disaster. You have the power to stop them. Extend compassion and love to yourself. You deserve it.

This is not a miracle cure rectified in a couple minutes. Some feelings may have been simmering for quite some time and may take a while to release. The important part is to begin the process. Look over your list each day, asking "What can I let go of today?" and "How will letting go of this allow my life to be more fulfilling and happier?"

The sting of each item on your list will lessen and begin to dissipate, and a void will be left in the place where negative feelings used to reside. This is a great time to replace that space with something positive. What do you really enjoy? Now's the time to take up that hobby or register for a course you've always wanted to do! Would you like to read, take a yoga class, learn to golf, garden, speak in public, volunteer, start a new business, learn to play an instrument? The possibilities are endless. Let your heart and mind wander to explore options you hadn't previously considered. Replace those old, worn out emotions that dull your senses and bring you down with exciting, sparkling practices that fill your heart with joy!

Again, I would like to mention that some of the items on your list may be so traumatic and hurtful they are best processed with a professional. Please don't minimize those experiences and feel like you "should" be able to handle them on your own. Don't be afraid to reach out and allow someone else to help. Releasing the hold they have over you and fully living your precious life is worth all the work. Really.

✦ Today's Step ✦

Think of a time when you were a complete idiot. You know what I'm talking about. You said something inappropriate to someone, you did something hurtful -- you were not living the highest and best version of yourself. Now, forgive yourself; and let it go. Truly let it go. You don't have to rationalize it, explain it, atone for it – just let it go and move on. Take a deep breath. Doesn't that feel awesome? Have a great day!

Patricia Shares Her Story

"Is it possible to obtain beauty out of the ashes of shattered dreams, joy out of sorrow, and peace out of adversity? What happens to the bitterness that comes from all of the pain and suffering?

It seems like anytime something awful happened to me I would flashback to being molested at six years old, being raped at sixteen. I didn't date much because the possibility of pain was too scary. When I met my now ex-husband, I saw someone that was kind, considerate, caring, and gentle. I decided he was the one that I would marry. He will take care of me. We will have a family. I will be a wife and mother, and live happily ever after. But soon came the silence. He wanted pornography more than me. He worked long hours. I was too busy with the kids. As always, I had this voice that blamed me. I must work harder, give more, and do everything better.

Married for 30 years, with four children, we appeared to be a normal, happy family, very busy, lots of activities, no real big problems. I often felt lonely. I would share how I was feeling and ask him what he thought. He would say, "Everything's fine. Everything's great. I'm happy." Then there must be something wrong with me. I must work harder, do things better. My whole life I felt like I could never do enough. I could never do it right. It wasn't good enough. The more I tried to please him, the emptier I became.

One summer weekend he joined a group of work colleagues on a business trip. I wasn't comfortable about it. I couldn't understand why he didn't invite me to join him. Sunday morning a small voice told me "You must meet him at the airport tonight. It will be a nice surprise to welcome him home." It was a surprise all right. A surprise for me when I saw him walking through the airport arm and arm with another woman, laughing, kissing, and hugging.

The day after I discovered the affair, God gave me the verses from Ephesians 3:14 to 21. "For this reason I've been on my knees before the father, from whom every family in heaven and on earth is named, that according to the riches of his glory he may grant you to be strengthened with power through his Spirit in your inner being, so that Christ may dwell in your hearts through faith – that you, being rooted and grounded in love, may have strength to comprehend with all the saints what is the breadth and length and the height and the depth, and to know the love of Christ that surpasses knowledge, that you may be filled with all the fullness of God. Now to him who is able to do far more abundantly than all that we may ask or think, according to the power at work within us, to him be the glory."

My life was shattered. My body was numb. The only thing I felt was pain. I needed to be strong for my kids. How would we ever make it through this nightmare? Nothing made sense or felt right, except the messege from Ephesians that God would grant me strength, power, and comprehension. I felt unloved and without purpose. It's all gone, been taken away and I had no choice. The verse says I will know the love of Christ and it surpasses all knowledge and I would be filled with His fullness. Everything seemed like a lie. I felt like an empty shell with no life. God said He's able to do more abundantly than I could ask or think.

The verses became my lifeline – the one truth I could hold onto.

It has been over four years since I discovered the affair, six times of giving him a chance to work things out. The day finally came that I could do no more; it was way past time for me to let go of my dream to be married. The lies needed to stop and the truth needed to be accepted. He did not want me, he did not love me. It wasn't my fault and there was nothing I could do to change it. I was now at a crossroad. Was I going to let the hurt and the pain of the past determine what my future would be, or was it time for me to discover "who am I?" My journey began with hours spent in counseling, journaling, crying, searching, believing, writing things down, burning them, and letting go. I carried the pain and fear of my past for so long all my thoughts were being filtered through lies, not the truth.

I began to forgive myself and others. The bitterness disappeared. I was able to live by faith and not fear. I took off my mask and let the secrets out that I had hidden away for so long. I began to be real and let the truth in.

I have discovered it is okay to take care of myself and do things that are good for me without worrying about what others might think or say. I have gained confidence and courage. I am not afraid to be me. I was not a failure, I was not worthless, I do have purpose.

God has made something beautiful from the ashes of shattered dreams. He has brought joy from the sorrow and given me peace from adversity. Great is His faithfulness! I am experiencing freedom and abundance I never imagined possible.

Each day is a new beginning. Embrace it with passion and make a difference!"

If you'd like to comment or share your own story with Tricia, please visit *www.ThePathThatBeckons.com.*

Chapter 3

The Path of Accepting
and Letting Go

"It takes a lot more courage to let something go than it does to hang on to it, trying to make it better. Letting go doesn't mean ignoring a situation. Letting go means accepting what is, exactly as it is, without fear, resistance, or a struggle for control."
– Iyanla Vanzant

My dad was not much of a traveler. He rarely ventured far from the small town he was born and raised in. He didn't need to, as five of his ten brothers and sisters lived within walking distance, and three were a short two-hour drive away.

One year my brother, Tony, convinced him to join him in Las Vegas for Super Bowl weekend. My dad reluctantly agreed to what would become an annual event both men looked forward to each year. Uncle Frank, my dad's brother, even joined the festivities a time or two.

This one weekend a year my dad, who lived a typically modest lifestyle, allowed himself to be pampered and live the good life. They stayed in a fancy suite at the Bellagio Resort and attended a private Super Bowl party. (Let's just say my brother has connections.) It was a special time for the two of them who were not only father and son, but best friends.

The year after my dad's death, my brother took my Uncle Frank again for their special weekend hoping to keep that precious memory alive, but it wasn't the same. They had fun, but the most important component for my brother was missing – our dad. After that year, Tony viewed the weekend completely differently. He realized the door had closed on that precious moment in time, and that part of his life was over forever. Instead of trying to recreate it or "make it work," he knew he was better off treasuring those memories in his heart and moving on.

I learned a valuable lesson from my insightful brother. He said the "seasons" in our lives. Just like the four seasons in a year, our lifetime seasons are here for a time and then they're gone. We create frustration and pain for ourselves when we don't recognize those periods and let go when they're over. Our human nature wants to hold on tight, refusing to move into the next season, whatever that may be. It doesn't mean we don't hold them in our minds and hearts and give thanks for them; we just know it's time to let go.

Is there something right now you're desperately clinging to even though you know it's over? Are you white-knuckling your life, believing if you hold on tight enough and long enough you can turn the situation around? I'm not advocating if the going gets tough you simply give up trying to repair or rectify the situation. Not at all. I believe in staying engaged and working toward a solution, whether it is in your marriage, your job, struggles with your children, whatever difficulty you're facing at the time.

Deep down we all know when we've given it all we have to give and it's time to let go. Whether we do or not is our choice. Guilt, shame, embarrassment, appearing weak, whatever your story is, there is something keeping you stuck in a season that has passed. That wiser part of you gently gives you a nudge, reminding you it's time to look ahead to the upcoming season. We don't always want to listen, even when we know it's true. The thing about an undesirable situation is, even though it's bad, we've probably learned how to maneuver around it; and, in participating in that dance, we continually try to convince ourselves it's not *that* bad. Moving into the unknown can appear scarier than where we are now because it's unchartered territory. Many times we opt for the familiar sad situation we're in over the unknown, even if there's a very real possibility of it providing us with an incredible life we will love.

I invite you to take a look at your journey in life, remembering that nothing is perfect. The path is cluttered with upsets, problems, and situations that challenge us every day. I'm not referring to the stumbling blocks that are the normal part of life. I want you to take a closer look at what's showing up right now. Is there a situation your heart of hearts has told you is finished and it's time to move on? Does it feel too big of a leap to do something about? Don't worry. I'm not going to encourage you to make that huge shift in your life right this second. I'd just like you to acknowledge it; and take the first step to reconciling to the fact that this might very well be the end of a season.

That step alone will shift something within you ever so slightly to allow the possibility of making that change. Be gentle with yourself. It probably took a while to get to where you are in your life. It will take time to make a change. A good intention to adopt is to be open to growing into the person who has the strength and ability to change their life, one small step at a time. And, as I always recommend, get help when you need it. There are people equipped to assist you in whatever situation you're going through.

I am reminded of the Serenity Prayer that most of us have heard or read: "God, grant me the serenity to accept the things I cannot change, courage to change the things I can, and wisdom to know the difference."

Accept the things I cannot change. That's the tough part for me. I want to be able to change everything... NOW! I guess that's part of my controlling nature.

I think if I try hard enough, work hard enough, or stress out enough, things will change. Sadly, that's usually not how it goes. In the end I find myself exhausted, discouraged, and emotionally spent. And guess what? The situation remains. In many cases, only when I've run out of options, am I able to let go and accept things as they are. Wouldn't it be easier and less stressful to be able to accept things before going through all that craziness?

I used to view accepting or letting go as passive and weak. I still have a bit of a negative charge when I hear the word surrender. To me, it conjures up an image of me on the floor face down with my cousin sitting on my back, pulling my leg up towards my head, while telling me to "Give up! Surrender!" In lieu of the word surrender, I find it easier to embrace the terms "letting go" and "acceptance." These terms lead me to believe I'm making a conscious decision, not simply giving in to default (or defeat). I'm choosing to accept what is. I'm choosing to let go. I feel empowered; and, yes, it may even appease my ego a bit.

Is there a condition in your life right now you can choose to accept just as it is, even if it doesn't look the way you want it to? What about that person in your life who you'd be happier being around if they were just a little bit different? Can you accept them just as they are? Accepting something or someone just as they are doesn't mean you don't have boundaries. You may accept them just as they are, but not want to spend time with or live with them. You may also accept them just as they are, but not be in business with them.

Okay, it's time to get to work again.

- Make a list of someone you have a hard time accepting just as they are.

- Next to their name, indicate one thing about them you wish they'd change. Or maybe there are several things about them that get under your skin.

- What if they never change? Can you imagine yourself accepting them as is?

- If you require particular boundaries to be okay with that decision, what are some you can implement? (An extreme example is to never interact with them again.)

Now make a second list.

- This time list one less than desirable reality of your life you're having a hard time accepting.

- What specifically about this instance do you wish were different? Is there anything within your power you can do for a real transformation in this area?

- Are you willing to take those steps accepting this situation may never change? Listen to your heart. If it's telling you this may never change, can you accept it as it is?

- What boundaries do you need to implement to be okay?

Determine the next best step for you, whether it's focusing your effort and energy, letting go, or accepting what is. It is a question only you can answer. My hope is you spend some time honestly contemplating the people and events in your life that require some attention. Listen to that quiet voice within that always tells you the truth and move forward into the appropriate season in your life. Maybe it's time to take off the snow boots and gloves to experience the flowers blooming and the robin's song. Or maybe you'll continue building snowmen for a while still. It's all up to you.

👣 Today's Step 👣

Refer back to the person on your first list. You did the exercise, right? If their situation is complex, maybe you can pick someone a little easier, a person in your life that only has a little quirk about them that's hard to accept. Now, come up with three things about them you like or three good qualities they possess. Resist the urge to say there's nothing about them to like. There's something to appreciate about everyone. If you're feeling really loving, play this game with everyone you meet today. You may be surprised how your perception of people changes by practicing this exercise!

Anne Shares Her Story

"Back in the late 1990s I had the opportunity of meeting and developing a friendship with an elderly woman, Marjorie. A neighbor approached me asking if I would mind helping out this fragile, sweet, little old lady by paying her bills, running to the store, and visiting with her once a week. I agreed, probably more out of not wanting to say no. I mean, how hard could it be?

My neighbor was right about the fact that she was little. She was in her mid-seventies and weighed a mere 72 pounds. Although she was a lady, she was anything but fragile or sweet. Marjorie was feisty, bawdy, and swore like a sailor! She kept me in stitches with the funny things she'd come up with.

I never spent any amount of time with a person of this age other than my grandparents when I had been a child. I saw them as most children do – Grandma and Grandpa. This interaction with Marjorie was different. She was a young woman trapped in an old body, a frail exterior housing a young and vibrant spirit. It made me a little sad as I faced the realization that this would happen to me one day as well.

Marjorie had experienced her share of pain in her life. Granted, she may have been the source of it, like racing around in her red convertible, smoking a cigarette in a long holder, much to the chagrin of her conservative parents. According to her, she was a disappointment and embarrassment to her family. She lived most of her life as a divorcee and was now a lonely recluse in an apartment complex, convinced everyone was out to get her. I think that was partly because she was quite wealthy from money she inherited from her family. Many times while writing out her bills she'd say she was concerned about running out of money. She'd ask, "Honey, what is my balance?" I don't think she ever called me by my name. It was always "Honey." I'd giggle to myself as I reported, "I think you're going to be fine. It's over $80,000." She'd laugh and say, "Okay. I guess I'm good until I get my check next month."

My once-a-week visit turned into three times a week, minimum. When it was time to go, she would conveniently recall "just one more thing" she'd like me to do. I accompanied her on her doctor's office visits and gladly assumed the role as her advocate and voice, to which she was very appreciative.

Her weekly shopping list usually included a bottle of Malibu Rum because it seemed to "help settle her stomach," and hamburger with lots of fat in it, "not the healthy kind."

A month or so before her death while I was at her apartment paying bills, she asked me to make out a check to myself for $10,000. I'm sure she knew she was approaching the end of her life, and she wanted to give it to me as a gift. I thankfully declined, saying we were friends; and I wasn't interested in her money. She insisted. She said she had already discussed it with her attorney and longtime friend, and told me to call him to verify. I spoke with the attorney who advised me to take the money because she was determined I have it; and we both knew there was no arguing with Marjorie. So I did as she asked. She signed the check.

I was with Marjorie at the care center the last few days leading up to her death. Her attorney contacted her estranged son with news that she would probably not make it through the night. He came to see her. When he arrived, I left them to their long overdue time alone and went home. I got the call during the night. My eclectic, quirky, ornery, precious friend was gone.

A few weeks later, I received a call from an officer from the local police department. He said Marjorie's son informed them that I stole $10,000 from his mother; and he would like to ask me a few questions. I naively agreed to come to the police station because I had nothing to hide. I thought I would explain the situation, have them contact the attorney for verification, and we'd be done.

I went directly to the police station. It did not go as I had expected. I was in an interrogation room for five hours, as they kept telling me to admit that I forged her signature and stole the money.

I explained over and over. I asked them to call Marjorie's attorney. He could verify everything. They refused; and I realized they had already made up their mind as to what had happened. Finally, they allowed me to go home, but only after the humiliation of a mug shot and fingerprinting. It was so deeply disturbing that I have no words to describe this surreal event. As I walked out, clearly shaken, the harsh interrogating officer sarcastically added, "Don't worry. The charges will probably be dropped."

I didn't hear anything at all after that, so I put it out of my mind and resumed my normal routine. Then one day, three months later, I was at the Department of Real Estate renewing my license. After pulling up my information, the clerk asked me to have a seat for a minute. Puzzled, I agreed. A few minutes later, in walked two uniformed policemen who headed directly towards me. They asked me to verify my name, which I did. Then they asked me to stand up as they handcuffed me. Right there in the real estate office! I was flabbergasted, asking them what was going on. They said there was a warrant for my arrest. I was going to jail. They took me in the back of a squad car to the jail, where I was allowed to call my husband to post bond. Everything was blurry. I felt like I was outside my body watching this situation unfold and thinking, What the ---?

I learned Marjorie's son was pressing charges, so I retained an attorney who was confident this would be dismissed immediately. I wasn't so sure. The steps that occurred in this process so far left me with little faith in the system. I thought that if you tell the truth, that would be that.

I was an emotional wreck, feeling humiliated and devalued. I don't remember ever stealing anything in my entire life, not even a piece of candy from a store as a kid. I internalized it and took it all very personally.

My court date for the preliminary hearing quickly approached. The judge would decide if there was enough evidence to move forward with a trial. I would now have to sit and look at the judgmental glances of the police officer, attorneys, judge, and random people in the courtroom. I didn't know how I was going to handle this without breaking down. I didn't want to do that.

What happened next made all the difference in the world.

As I sat on the bench outside the courtroom trying to gain my composure and breathe normally, I said a silent prayer. Lord, you know I didn't do this, and that's all that matters. I've done everything I know to do so far to reveal the truth. There is nothing more for me to do, so I let *go and turn it over to you. At that point, I let go of my feelings attached to this situation. I let go of the negative feelings I'd been holding against this misdirected son and the overzealous police officer. I let go of holding onto what was about to happen. I let go of the outcome. I let go of it all. And instead, I trusted. I trusted it would all work out perfectly.*

It felt like a hundred pounds had been lifted from my shoulders. I breathed a sigh of relief and I felt at peace. Really at peace.

I walked into the courtroom where it began. The prosecutor called the interrogating officer to the stand. I did not bow my head in embarrassment. I calmly and confidently looked directly into his eyes. I locked eyes with him throughout his entire testimony, even as I listened to his degrading accusations.

It was now my attorney's turn to ask the questions. As he arose, the judge stopped him short. He was not allowed to ask anything. The judge's response was, "I've made a decision. Nothing you can ask or say that would change it." My attorney pled with him to allow him the opportunity to speak, but the judge stayed firm. My attorney shot me a look that said, "This is not good."

The judge announced he would be back in a few minutes. We waited in silence.

Upon his return, the judge dismissed the case. He said he didn't need to hear anything more. There was no evidence that I'd done anything wrong. If Miss Marjorie wanted to give me a gift, it was her right.

The outcome would probably have been the same had I surrendered or not. Or would it? Maybe the confidence and ease I exhibited as a result of releasing allowed me to show who I really am. I'll never know. I don't need to. What was pivotal for me, and what I will always remember from this situation, was the unbelievable shift that took place in my soul when I let go. That simple act of surrender and acceptance made all the difference in the world for me."

If you'd like to comment or share your own story with Anne, please visit *www.ThePathThatBeckons.com.*

Part 2

Stepping Onto the Trail

Chapter 4

The Path of Being Present

"Right now is the most important moment in your life."
– Gail Lynne Goodwin

Some people spend a great deal of their waking hours focused on the past. This may come in the form of replaying an unpleasant situation or conversation, regretting a decision, thinking about "what might have been," or reliving their glory days. Regardless of whether the memory is good or bad, it elicits an emotion. And even though the incident may have happened twenty years ago, the emotion created is as vivid as if it were occurring right now. The brain's funny that way.

I reflect on things from time to time, but wouldn't say I invest a lot of energy there. I, on the other hand, spend many of my waking hours focused on the future. I like to plan. I make goals, set intentions, plan vacations or adventures, and spend time setting up processes and steps to achieve those aspirations. I used to feel a bit self-righteous about the fact that I don't spend my time submerged in the past. I prefer to look to the future. I'm a dreamer; and that's what dreamers do, right?

Then one day a harsh realization hit me. Focusing time and energy on the future is no different from focusing on the past. Both activities prevent you from living in the present.

Revisiting your past to deal with and heal from a hurtful experience or painful event is not only valuable, but necessary to move forward in a positive, powerful way in your life. There is a difference in looking back to delve into your past for the purpose of healing versus looking back to rehash negative situations, replay arguments, or stoke the fire of resentment.

By the same token, looking ahead, making plans, and creating steps to improve your life are also worthwhile. This process provides direction, creates enthusiasm, and generates happiness and growth in life.

The key here is to take a look at how much time you spend in either of these places. If you are continually dwelling in the past or in the future, you may be oblivious to what's happening right here, right now.

I participated in a weekend self-improvement course about twenty years ago. I don't remember much of the content of that course, but one small aspect made an indelible impression on me. Every morning when beginning the session, as well as after every lunch and miscellaneous break, the course started the same way. The leader would encourage us to leave our conversations at the door, let go of any concerns or outside worries, and be present. The words used to convey this message were the same: *"Be here now."*

I continue to use that simple reminder in various situations when my mind starts to wander away from where I am. When I recognize I'm not in the conversation or situation, I gently remind myself, *"Be here now."*

Sitting in my quiet time alone this morning, I asked myself, (yes, I talk to myself) *Why would I choose to distract myself by shifting my focus and energy on another time rather than living fully in the present? What's wrong with the present?* I was surprised by what instantly bubbled up.

Immediately, I was flooded with emotions. The first was fear, the kind where your heart races and your palms sweat. You know – the one of feeling real impending danger. A few weeks ago a strange man came to my door during the day when I was home alone. I didn't answer and a few minutes later I caught sight of a different man carrying a crowbar on my patio walking toward my back door. He saw me and ran away, fleeing by jumping over my back fence. I immediately called 911 and both men were apprehended. The next couple days I was jumpy and nervous, but I got over it, or so I thought. My rational mind reminded me I was very lucky with the way things turned out and any perceived danger had passed. The situation unfolded perfectly with a safe ending; and I hadn't given it much thought since then. Until now. The moment I turned my focus to truly being present, that unresolved feeling of fear for my personal safety reappeared.

The next emotion I felt was exasperation. I felt angry with myself for gaining weight. Last summer I worked hard to get close to my ideal weight and felt healthy, optimistic, and good about myself. Over the past ten months I allowed the weight to slowly creep back on. To me, this equalled so many things to be mad at myself about – lack of control, lack of self-respect, lack of determination. Shame on me.

The third emotion was sadness. Now I was feeling guilty for the brutal, unforgiving way I relate to myself, and for being in this familiar place again. This range of emotions drained me, leaving me disempowered and weak.

So, how was that for an answer to being in the now? Pretty hefty emotions, but also an interesting observation about being present all from a few minutes of checking in with myself.

Maybe the reason we spend time in the past or future is to distract ourselves from dealing with what's screaming for our attention in the present. It appears I have some work to do myself as I venture down the *Path of Being Present*.

I encourage you to try a similar experience. Situate yourself in a quiet place and ask if there's anything keeping you from living fully in the present. Truly listen. Are there unresolved feelings you're carrying that, if you were able to let go of, being present would be fun and fulfilling and make your path more joyful?

I'll admit that I'm an avoider. I don't particularly care for conflict or dealing with uncomfortable feelings or situations. I want everyone to be happy and get along. What I am learning is that in life conflict is normal. However, I don't have to let it consume me. I can choose to be open to resolve conflict in an amicable way where I'm understanding and respectful of the other person, as well as to myself. Uncomfortable feelings and situations are also a part of life I am still learning to be okay with. I find there is typically a valuable lesson in these situations, and moving through them, allowing myself to fully experience what I need to, transports me to a place of deeper understanding of myself.

As with anything worth value, it takes some work. Taking a look to see if there's something that makes living in the present unappealing is the first step. Once you recognize what's stopping you, you have the opportunity of working through it to be fully engaged and joyously captivated in the right here – right now.

So, are you ready to take that first step? Are you being called to live more fully each day? What would that look like for you?

What if you got up in the morning, refrained from making a list of your daily activities while simultaneously responding to emails, and quickly downing your morning coffee? What if, instead, you pour a steamy fresh cup of coffee into your favorite mug, the one that feels perfect in your hand? You slowly inhale the aroma with your eyes closed and appreciate the moment. You make your way to your favorite comfy chair, sit back, put your feet up, and snuggle with your cozy throw. As you fully relax, you take the first sip of your coffee, savoring the flavor and warmth of the steamy drink as it makes its way down your body. You take a deep breath, look around your room, and think of all you have to feel happy about in this moment.

I hear the naysayers already lamenting, "I don't have time for that. I have to work. I have responsibilities. I don't have time to sit around." I get it. I really do. But do you realize this experience takes a total of less than ten minutes? Ten minutes to center yourself and fully embrace the present moment. I'll bet you can take ten minutes.

Then throughout the day, pause for a moment. You can use my mantra and silently say to yourself, "Be here now," or you can look around and connect with your senses. What are you aware of that you haven't noticed before? What sounds do you hear? Is there a faint, pleasant scent you almost missed? How are you feeling? What is your heart saying to you right now?

Give it a try. Create your own practice to stay connected to the present. Remember, it's your life, your path, and your reality. Make it unique. Make it awesome!

◄⋅✦ Today's Step ◄⋅✦

Designate a time today to turn your cell phone off. I hear the gasps of panic from some of you already, and even a few, "Oh, hell, no's." It will be okay. I promise. Just shut them off for an hour. Maybe while you're in the car. Instead of checking voice mail, making calls, and texting (hopefully while stopped at the red lights), listen to your favorite radio station or a CD. Really listen. Better yet, sing along! Relax and unplug for a few minutes to fully be aware of this amazing world we live in. I have faith in you. You can do it!

Maraion Shares Her Story

"As I began to live in the present eight years ago, after resigning from my position with American Express to chase my dream of opening the doors of MOMA's house, a safe house for women who have been victims of abuse, I was scared. In order to face the task that God had given me, I had to revisit the past, something that I had suppressed for over twenty years. Instead of dwelling in the past and on all the mistakes I made, I had to live in the present because it was not all about me.

It took the pain from the past to shield the challenges that I was going to face in the present without fully knowing what the future held. As I began my new journey, I came to the understanding that the life I lived prepared me for what God was calling me to do.

There were so many times in the beginning of the journey when I had flashbacks of things I experienced in the past, but kept well tucked away in a safe place. I thought. The pain was sometimes unbearable and somewhat unbelievable. I was so angry with myself because I allowed myself to be treated like that. I gave my husband at the time control of my life when it was my life. So in a way, I was a part of the abuse, self-abuse. I was often told, "You made your bed so lay in it." What does that mean? No, I am not going to wallow in this. Instead, I am going to get up, dust myself off, and keep moving. I was not going to continue to be a victim of domestic violence. I was a survivor and I had two children that needed me to be just that. And so I did!

The present has been such an amazing gift to me regardless of the trials and tribulations I have experienced. By surrendering all to God, I have been able to not only witness miracles, but to realize that I am a miracle. God has provided me with 'angels along the way.' He strategically placed people in my life because he knew I would need their support and unconditional love.

The road I am traveling has been one of many disappointments, second guessing myself, and still trying to please all. There have been many times that I wanted to just give up and go back to what was safe for me. I began to question myself, Are you really being a difference, creating a difference, or showing a difference in the lives of the women that have walked through the doors of MOMA's house? I even entertained the thoughts and negative conversations from others who questioned it as well. I began to travel back to the past, but God said to me, "I have given you a gift, Maraion. It is called the present. I am with you; and I will never forsake you." So that is my daily confirmation that I am doing what I was born to do.

When we live in the present, each day is a new day indeed. It is a new opportunity to walk the walk and not just talk the talk. It is an opportunity to fill a void in a life, put a smile on a face, and show unconditional love as God shows us. It is an opportunity to enjoy the things that so many take for granted, even though you know it can be gone in a blink of an eye. It is like the Red Sea parting all over again because you are leaving all your fears behind and traveling to a place of peace, the kind of peace that only God can give to you in the present.

As I continue my journey, I am grateful that it has allowed me to be the best that I can be. It has shown me *that my present is much greater than my past, and the future is God smiling like a sunrise!*

Many blessings."

For more information on Maraion's organization, to provide support, or to contact her, please visit *www.ThePathThatBeckons.com.*

Chapter 5

The Path of Hope

"Don't worry about a thing, 'cause every little thing gonna be all right."
– Bob Marley

Just the other day, I was sitting in my favorite "thinking about stuff" chair relaxing after finishing my morning prayer and meditation time. My husband has a straw hat he wears while working in the yard and the grandkids call it his "doing stuff" hat. I think it's only fair that I have a "thinking about stuff" chair, and there I sat.

As I gazed out the large windows in my living room, I saw the familiar view I am blessed with every day: a huge mesquite tree straight ahead in our back yard; another big billowy tree similar to a weeping willow to its right; with an old dead tree between the two that has been repurposed as our

Wind Chime tree, holding various music-makers (usually Christmas gifts from the little ones) creating a beautiful melody when a breeze passes through. A flurry of activity in the yard is the norm. There's a constant flow of birds flying in, landing on one of the tree branches, then getting on their way to some unknown adventure. My favorite bird is a vibrant red cardinal who makes an occasional appearance. Since I'm in Arizona, I'm also treated to cactus wrens, woodpeckers, hummingbirds, quail, and an occasional roadrunner darting across the lawn. And let's not forget the lizards and chipmunks. It's like a wild animal preserve at times!

Today was different. It was completely still. Not a breeze in the air. The trees and wind chimes were eerily motionless, as if frozen in time. I watched for a few seconds entranced by the stillness. This couldn't last long, right? I looked at the time on the clock and decided to see how long this phenomenon could continue. It was a bit weird that everything could be so still, so I began to concentrate more intensely. Surely one leaf would have a slight sway, but no. And not a bird to be found. As closely as I could focus on this unusual moment in time, nothing changed for ten minutes. Perfect stillness for ten minutes! Then an ever so slight breeze swirled in that was just enough to cause a leaf on the mesquite tree to stir.

Contemplating that experience reminded me life is typically in constant motion whether we're talking about nature, energy, animals, or people. When motion ceases, even for ten minutes, it feels unnatural and uncomfortable.

I recall times in my life when I felt stuck in a situation or in a place where I couldn't see the sunrise over the horizon. You know those times. Times when you've experienced something so painful you don't believe your heart will ever recover; and you can't imagine things ever getting better. There is a haunting stillness that carries with it overwhelming heavy-heartedness, gloom and despondency. To put it simply – you have no hope.

Have you been there? Are you there now? If so, please don't allow yourself to remain in this dark place any longer than you have to. Ask yourself what your soul needs to regain hope. Then do whatever it takes to get yourself out of this desolate space.

Let's try a little exercise to help you reclaim hope in your life.

- The first step is to be completely real with yourself. Look at what is causing your pain or current state of being. Be specific.

- Is this a situation you have power to do something about?

- If so, what steps can you take to restore your hope and shine a new light on your life?

If you're faced with a situation you have no control over and it just "is what it is," ask yourself, "What's good about this?" There has to be at least one thing.

Is it an opportunity for you to change something about yourself? Is it a chance to regain your power? Maybe it's time to come to terms and be at peace with something you're letting run your life. Really listen to the answer. Then make a decision to move forward, and take a step. Call a friend. Go for a walk. Create a gratitude list of the beauty in your life and what you have to feel happy about. Go see a fun, uplifting movie. It will, undoubtedly, be uncomfortable at first. You probably will have to force yourself back into motion, but it's worth the effort.

If you feel what you're experiencing is complex and more than you can deal with alone, please seek help. There is something very powerful about acknowledging you need help and taking the first step in that direction. You may want to seek the advice of a professional, become a member of a support group, or sit down in a heart to heart conversation with someone you trust.

To live a life of hopelessness is one of the saddest states I can imagine. I'm sure we all visit that den of doom from time to time depending on the situation we're going through. But the key is not to stay there. Hopelessness breeds more hopelessness, and before you know it, you'll find yourself in a deep pit that seems impossible to crawl out of. *Do not stay there!* Start digging your way out.

Challenge yourself to step out onto the promising *Path of Hope*.

Once hope is restored, the entire world shows up differently. You begin seeing everything with new eyes. The sky looks bluer, the stars brighter; you have a reason to get up in the morning.

From this new place of hope, you can dream about what you want in life and how to get there from where you are. This is when your juices start to flow. You envision your life in a new fresh way. Don't be surprised when powerful people, interesting situations, and exciting events begin to show up!

Growing up, when someone was physically ill or given a dire prognosis, my mother's hopeful advice was always, "Don't give up. Where there's life, there's hope." She's right. As long as you're breathing, your life can radically change in an instant. Health can be restored, relationships mended, new loving bonds formed, and businesses recharged. There is no limit to what your life can be, regardless of what your limited vision can see now.

Can you remember a time in when you couldn't see any possible way a negative situation you were in could change? You racked your brain for any and all possible solutions but nothing came to mind. Then out of the blue something happened that was so far outside your realm of possibilities you couldn't even imagine it. It was the perfect answer and the situation diffused. Now, granted, that doesn't happen every time; but when it does, it's a beautiful reminder we don't have to have all the answers. Sometimes we only have to maintain a belief that it can improve – hope.

Many times I am quick to sum up something as "bad" or "good." Instantly labeling it slams the door to possibilities. Mary Morrissey, life coach and motivational speaker, suggests we postpone labeling an event or situation for three days to let it play out. Something we initially perceive as "bad" may, in fact, bring a benefit to our life and actually be a blessing. She also states that instead of judging something as good or bad, let's ask ourselves how we can be empowered by what's happening. Not only are we keeping the door to hope fully open, we are also using this as an opportunity to grow from the experience. Try it out next time.

What are you hopeful about in your life? What area have you lost hope on, and are you willing to restore that hope? What steps can you implement to become a person, filled with hope, who inspires and encourages others to discover that refreshing spring for themselves?

Today's Step

Throughout the day, with each situation that comes up, ask yourself, "What's one thing good about this?" It can be something you've labeled as bad or good as it works both ways. This practice also applies to people. With every person you encounter or talk to today, ask yourself, "What's one thing good about them?" It just may shift how you see your world. Wouldn't that be a fun way to look at life? Put on your hope goggles!

Kristen shares her story

"When you get into a tight place and everything goes against you, till it seems as though you could not hang on a minute longer, never give up then, for that is just the place and time that the tide will turn." –Harriet Beecher Stowe

I love a new year. It brings with it an air of fresh possibilities, combined with the stability of the mundane. So it was for me as my little family and I rang in 2015 happy, healthy and full of excitement. My goals likely included a renewed interest in dropping some pounds, keeping up the house a little better, enjoying life a bit more, the usual. My life, by all accounts, was pretty perfect with my adoring husband and two beautiful sons, ages 6 and 3. What I didn't know is ten days into this new year, my pretty, perfect world would start crumbling before my eyes. 2015 would quickly become the hardest, darkest year of my life.

Our 3 year old son, Jayden, began having seizures. They came on suddenly without any reason. We took him to the closest children's hospital. I truly expected the doctors to tell us that things like this happen on occasion and all would be fine. Quite the opposite became our reality. Jayden was diagnosed with epilepsy. Over the next three months, my happy, healthy son would deteriorate to a screaming child who would alternate being a child with a blank stare and no response to one who literally would throw himself down our staircase. We would later find out it was a side effect of the medication. Months went on, as did the medication changes, seizures, more side effects and no hope from the doctors as to when this would end, if this would end and if we would get our bright, cheerful son back without any permanent damage to his development.

My perfect world had ended. My light went dark. I cried out in the darkness, but all I heard back was a deafening silence. I began to grieve the loss of my son as I had known him. My faith had been easy to live out, until now. Where was this God whom I adored, the One which I believed loved my son even more than I? I certainly could not easily see Him, so I knew in my heart that I had to actively seek Him. However, that required energy which I did not have.

At the beginning of April, everything seemed to be falling apart even more. I began to feel alone, began to give in to the darkness around me, and it was anything but pretty. Fortunately, this feeling scared me. I decided to pray specifically for a glimmer of hope, a sign, anything to know that Jayden mattered to God, that I mattered to Him, that my family mattered to Him. "Oh, my Father, I need hope. I need to see You." It was quick. It was simple, but it was all I could muster in the middle of watching my baby boy now progress into grand mal seizures which would last 4 or 5 minutes, often multiple times a day. I decided that I would pray this prayer over and over, day after day, until my heart was satisfied that we did matter, that the One who created me, the one that created Jayden, the one who I was taught cares about each sparrow in the sky, decided to show up and let me see with my own eyes that my son mattered, that I mattered, that God cared and was going to help me get through this. "Oh, my Father, I need hope. I need to see You."

I felt that my prayer was never to be answered. Things continued to get worse for Jayden. I realized that I began to disconnect from life. Yet, I continued to pray my simple prayer, and day by day, the words rang even more true. "Oh, my Father, I need hope. I need to see You." A friend was leaving to do a huge walk in Spain called Camino de Santiago. I sent her a quick message asking her to light a prayer candle along her path for Jayden, half hoping she would, half wondering why she would even think of us on this huge journey. I followed her journey each day through her blog. It became an escape from my reality. On Mother's Day, I had mustered up enough energy to go to church. When we left, I had a message to make sure I read her blog, as it was for me. She hadn't found a place to light a candle, a place "worthy", in her words, "of an intimate prayer of a mother." Her words went on to touch my soul in a way that I so desperately needed. She had no idea, but she was the sign I had been praying God would send me. Her words were what I had needed, what I had longed for, what I had cried for. This friend was walking around 15 miles per day, but she took the time on her journey to think of me. Her words were truly a gift from my Heavenly Father. She was detailed in writing what she felt this journey I was on would bring, she pointed out the good things that I needed to see, that I had a ton of people who genuinely loved me, and loved my family. Then, she painted a picture with her words of my Heavenly Father holding Jayden in His arms, reassuring me that He loves Jayden more than I. She encouraged me that His arms are not only around Jayden's, but around all four of us and that I needed to lean on Him and trust in that knowledge.

Her note was truly a turning point for me. It was exactly what I needed to ignite my light of hope, that the God of the Universe, my Heavenly Father, was indeed there with me and with Jayden. That tangible knowledge gave me wings to soar, gave me the courage to start questioning the medical treatment for Jayden and ultimately led us to a different medical team, strategically selected by my husband and I, which has given us even more hope, that Jayden will be completely healed and off of his medication at least before the end of 2016.

My path of hope continues to be dark at times, but I have an understanding that it is truly in the darkest of times when you do come to appreciate the Light.

If you'd like to comment or share your own story with Kristen, please visit *www.ThePathThatBeckons.com.*

Chapter 6

The Path of Courage

"Life shrinks or expands in proportion to one's courage."
– Anais Nin

What images appear in your mind where you hear the word "courage?" Is it a firefighter rescuing a frightened child from a burning building? A soldier telling their concerned family goodbye in an airport? Or a small group of people joining together to stand up for the rights of many?

The word "courage" in and of itself seems almost larger than life. "The quality of mind or spirit that enables a person to face difficulty, danger, pain, etc. without fear" is how *www.dictionary.com* defines the word. The part that throws me off about this definition is "without fear." Do you believe courageous people don't experience fear? I don't.

I believe a courageous person has the internal fortitude to face difficulty, danger, or pain not without fear, but *in spite of* fear.

We all experience fear. It's how we respond that determines if we're courageous or not. Fear can be a crippling emotion if we allow it. It can stop us dead in our tracks. You know that dream we've all had where we sense something dangerous behind us; but because of fear we're not able to run to safety or even look back to see what it is? It may not be just a dream. Are there times or situations in your life where fear has literally paralyzed you and you've remained right where you were instead of taking the next step in life because it felt too scary?

What stops you from exemplifying courage? What fear has a grip on you? Are you afraid of failure? Are you afraid of success?

Reading these two questions out loud sounds silly, but it's a great exercise to help you gain clarity. You may understand a fear of failure, but why would anyone be afraid of success? As much as we don't like to fail and we feel embarrassed by it, deep down we know it is part of life; and everyone fails at one time or another. But success – now that's a different story. When you succeed, you open up a whole different can of worms. Are people going to be jealous and perceive you as thinking you're better than them now? Will your success make your friends and family uncomfortable? And what about your own uneasiness in this unfamilar realm? Will success set you apart or draw unwanted attention you're not used to?

Which fear is more prevalent for you – fear of failure or fear of success? Are you willing to move forward, regardless of which has the tighter grip as we bravely venture down the *Path of Courage*?

Courage is like a muscle, the more you flex it, the stronger it becomes. Looking back on your life, were there things twenty years ago that you couldn't fathom yourself doing; but now you don't give them a thought as they've almost become second nature?

Take speaking or presenting to a group of people, for example. Maybe you were extremely shy and just the thought of an oral presentation would cause your heart to race and your palms to sweat. Then one day your best friend asks you to offer a toast at her upcoming wedding. Fear immediately bubbles to the surface and you want to say no. But you can't do that to your best friend. It's her wedding. So you rehearse what you'll say to say so many times you can recite it in your sleep. You remind yourself it's a small wedding and you know most of the people there. You convince yourself you can do it. And you do! Yes, you had sweaty palms; and, yes, your voice cracked once. But you were the only one to notice. You made it through the experience. The next time something like this came up, it got a little easier. You realized it didn't kill you the first time, and continued practicing whenever you had the opportunity. Before you knew it, you were speaking in front of people on a regular basis. You may still have experienced the sweaty palm syndrome, but you kept moving forward in spite of the apprehension.

Where is fear holding you back right now? What area in your life would you like to display more courage? It's doesn't have to be a huge undertaking. One thing that holds me back and keeps me afraid is the fear of what people think of me. I know it's silly. Who cares, right? Well, apparently I do.

In junior high school, I developed a love of writing. My English teacher, Mrs. Milovich, not only introduced me to the concept of journaling, but provided the encouragement for me to bravely document my deepest thoughts and feelings. I connected wholeheartedly with this new method of expressing myself without fear of others reading it or grading me on the content. I will always be grateful to her for that gift.

To this day, I journal regularly. Many times after writing, I tear the pages out and throw them away. The point is not to read what I write, but to express what I'm feeling and investigate deeper who I am and what I want in life.

I love to write, yet I am fully aware I'm nowhere near the same league as Elizabeth Gilbert. I read a quote once that said, "Don't write what people want to read. Write what's yours to say." I don't have anything earth-shattering or life-changing to impart, but I believe I share the same fears, joys, and emotions as most people. My sincere hope is to create a connection through words that inspire and encourage others to live their best lives.

A few years ago, I decided l would write a blog. I envisioned it being like my personal writings, except this time I would not only save them instead of tossing them out, but I would make them available for anyone to read. I was immediately consumed by fear. Was I ready to put myself out there and have my deepest thoughts revealed? I knew if I were to write, I would have to be transparent. I couldn't write superficially. I wanted to write what was in my heart. Turning yourself inside out onto paper is pretty intimidating. What if people don't like it? What if they think I'm stupid? I don't have a writing style, proper sentence structure, or punctuation. Who am I to think I can do this?

After my craziness subsided a bit in my head, one bold thought shouted louder than the rest, *Who cares?*

I recognized those negative thoughts as my ego reminding me to stay small; and it offered so many valid reasons. But I didn't listen. I just did it. Was I scared? Hell, yes. Did I hope everybody liked it? I'm embarrassed to say this; but, yes, I did. Did they? Probably not, even though I didn't receive any harsh comments. Yet, in the scheme of things, what if they had voiced negative responses? Would it have mattered enough for me to stop? Nope!

At this point, you may be thinking, *Really? Writing a blog is her biggest fear? Pshaw.* It may not be my biggest challenge; but it's easier to be brave in big situations when we've practiced with the small things. As we overcome and defeat little fears, we flex our courage muscles and are better equipped to face bigger obstacles as they present themselves.

One of my favorite people is Paulo Coelho, the author most famous for his book, *The Alchemist*. I enjoy his writing. But more than that, I am inspired by who he is as a person and his attitude about life. In an rare interview with Oprah Winfrey, published in the October 2014 issue of *O Magazine*, he shared the following story:

"About three years ago, I had heart surgery. I had gone in for a simple stress test and my doctors told me suddenly that I would die in 30 days without intervention. But I went home and was very relaxed. I thought, 'I'm going in for heart surgery. I may die tomorrow.' But then I realized that if I die tomorrow, I've spent more than half my life with the woman I love. How many people on this planet can say that? She's my fourth marriage, but we've spent 35 years together. And I tell her, 'I love you' every day. The second thing I thought is, 'I did everything. I was crazy. I went to extremes.' So I have nothing to regret, because I did everything. And the third thing I realized is that I fought for my dream. I did not take no for an answer. I wanted to be a writer, and I wrote. So I thought, 'If I die tomorrow, it's all okay.'"

When you're living a courageous life, you have nothing to regret. In fulfilling the purpose you came to this earth for, you step out to do what's yours to do in the face of fear. Fear will never completely subside, but you always have a choice. Ask yourself this question: "Do I want to let this fear stop me; or am I brave enough to move through this dark scary place of fear into the exhilarating light of living my dream and playing big?" Here are a few more questions to respond to as well:

- What's one area of your life you want to be more courageous in?

- What step can you take today to begin?

- Are you willing to let go of what others think of you in order to live a more purposeful and joyous life?

Stay on this path for a while, my friend, as you exercise your courage muscle and move into an amazing new realm of possibilities!

🐾 *Today's Step* 🐾

Think of one thing you're holding back from doing because you're afraid. This can be as small as calling a friend you haven't talked to in a long time, or as big as launching a new business. It's up to you. And, now just DO IT! If it feels too daunting, take a small piece of it and do that. You're always going to have fear. But decide today it doesn't get to rule your life. You're in charge – not fear! Did I just hear a roar?

Ruby's Story

Can you imagine being informed at the innocent age of fourteen that you're getting married very shortly, your selected spouse is in his twenties, AND your second cousin? Most of us are not even able to wrap our heads around this idea; but for Ruby and many girls like her, it's a somber reality. You see, Ruby grew up in the small polygamist community of Colorado City, which lies near the Arizona-Utah border. Her household consisted of multi-family units with twenty-six siblings.

The announcement of her upcoming union was not entirely a surprise, as this is the norm in that culture. Still, hearing those painful words condemning her to a life sentence with a man she didn't love, made Ruby angry and scared. Her emotions were simply wasted energy, as she had no say in the decision, no voice regarding her life whatsoever.

Two weeks before turning fifteen when most girls are planning a slumber party with her best gal pals to giggle about boys they like, Ruby got married.

On her wedding night, she was forcibly made to perform her "wifely duty." In the years that followed, Ruby says she never had consensual sex, always forced. By the time she was twenty-four, she had six children. Through these tragic and difficult years, it was her children who kept her going. She existed for them and gave them all the love she had in her tender, but wounded heart.

It was not in Ruby's nature to resign herself to this life. She was constantly devising plans in her head to escape, but that would be no easy task. She was under the constant watchful eyes of not only her husband, but the leaders of the church and the community, which included the police force. Besides, where could she find a job to support her and her children? Her eighth grade education surely would not get her far. But that didn't stop her. She kept thinking.

Ruby's sister, who had already separated herself from the community, was now an advocate and some say a vigilante for these young girls without a voice. She spoke out in the media; but even when the story grew old and interest moved onto the new topic of the day, she continued. She would sneak into town in the middle of the night rescuing young women with their children and taking them to safe havens far away from this nightmare. As soon as the town got wind of this, they tightened security and Ruby was not allowed to speak with her sister at all. They even randomly moved Ruby and her family around to different houses to prevent the sisters from connecting. Still Ruby didn't give up.

One day she asked if she could visit a friend in Canada. She was allowed to go, but not take her children. Everyone knew she would not leave her children. She would be back. And she did come back, but that was not her plan. Her plan was to get a job, save up some money, go back and fight for her kids, and move them to a new safe life. Unfortunately, she wasn't able to get a job that could support her, let alone six little mouths. She returned disheartened after a month to the children she so desperately missed and loved.

There were a couple other attempts, but she was either brought back or convinced by someone, who said they had her best interest in mind, to return.

Four months later she decided she had had enough. She knew she HAD to leave. She understood making this move meant any and all contact with her mother, step-father, siblings and friends would be forever severed. It was a price she had to pay. She didn't know how she would make it when she got out, but she didn't care. She summoned up all the courage she had and made plans to leave. One night in the shadows, she set out for Phoenix to be with her sister. At that point, she felt alone and defeated, thinking she had no rights to her children at all. But, she was about to find out how the law really worked. Her sister, Flora, assured her she DID have rights and together they would fight for all six of those precious little babies. After all, no mother leaves her children behind.

The sisters petitioned the courts for temporary emergency custody, and after what seemed like the longest month ever, Ruby and all six of her children were reunited in Phoenix.

Upon their safe arrival, Ruby and her sister immediately set about making her sister's single wide trailer a home for six more people. Beds were made on the sofa and all around the floor. Nobody minded. They were safe. They were together. They were free.

As you might guess, the story doesn't end here. The unbelievable amount of courage it took to leave Colorado City paled in comparison to the intense and ongoing bravery it took to make a new life in a world that was like a foreign country to Ruby. Everything she had done in the past, every part of her daily life, was regulated and mandated by someone else. As dysfunctional as this structure was, it provided a sense of security, albeit a false one. And, as much as she hated it, she knew it. She didn't know anything about where she was now.

Luckily, she didn't have to do it alone. There were people that heard Ruby's story, and the fact that she had taken a job at a gas station working the graveyard shift so she could be at home during the day with her kids. Many stepped up to help. People she'd never even met assisted Ruby in getting her family's basic needs met and eventually moving them into a small home of their own. She now works at a job with better hours and higher pay, and has her sights set on the next step, obtaining her GED.

The movie, "Cathedral Canyon" was made to bring awareness to this tragic (and illegal) treatment of girls most of us either don't know exists or find too painfully heartbreaking to acknowledge. Ruby fearlessly shares her personal story with strangers in hopes she can help other girls in her situation. She is sweet, open, and the kind of person you feel like you've known all your life from the minute you meet her. It's amazing that experiencing all she has in her short twenty-nine years hasn't hardened her.

When she wraps her arms around you for a hug that lasts a little longer than you may normally feel comfortable with, you are left with a knowing that's Ruby is going to be just fine. It won't be an easy road for her, but at least now **she** gets to decide how her life will look, not anyone else.

For more information on the organization or to provide support, or to comment or share your own story with Ruby, please visit *www.ThePathThatBeckons.com.*

Part 3

Embarking on a Pilgrimage

Chapter 7

The Path of Connection

*"Though free to think and act, we are held together, like
the stars in the firmament, with ties inseparable.
These ties cannot be seen, but we can feel them."*
– Nikola Tesla

My deepest connection with another human being was the moment my newborn daughter was laid into my arms. If you have given birth, you undoubtedly share this precious awareness. It is unlike any closeness I had known with another human being. This miniature person was quite literally connected to me, body to body, for nine months. My food and nutrients went into this forming child and we were one. Even after that tiny human was no longer cradled in my womb, the connection remained. How do we create and nurture a similar connection with other people in our lives, and do we want to?

Social media has drastically altered the way we connect with others. It allows me to stay in touch with friends and family clear around the world, especially those I probably would not keep in close contact with otherwise. The posts they share on Facebook allow a glimpse into their day-to-day world in a way an occasional phone call doesn't provide. It also offers an avenue to keep up with distant friends or colleagues I've lost touch with over time. With that said, it also offers to connect me with some people I purposely haven't kept in contact with. I guess that's why there's an"unfriend" button!

Even with the benefits social media provides, it's still a "distant" connection. It's not the method I use to communicate with family and friends who are most important in my life. For me to truly connect, I need to sit in front of someone, look into their eyes as they speak, hear the tone and inflection in their voice, watch their body language, and reach out to touch their hand occasionally or provide a hug when it feels appropriate. That is true connection for me. Words, spoken or written, are merely one part of an intimate conversation or connection.

When we experience pain, rejection, or abandonment, it's natural to want to protect ourselves from being in a hurtful situation again. No one wants that. In an effort to defend our heart, it may seem more convenient and less threatening to communicate through a distant method. We feel separated and a bit more in control. After all, we can push that "unfriend" button any time we feel confronted or unsure. Unfortunately, life doesn't come with a button to push that instantaneously removes a person who makes us feel unsafe or vulnerable. We are left to discover other ways to create that imaginary button for ourselves.

What ways do you protect yourself from connection with others in hopes of keeping yourself safe?

Maybe you are a "do-er" – someone who busies themselves to avoid getting out and meeting people. This can be a dangerous mode to get into and may manifest itself in a couple ways.

The first way is to busy (or distract, because that's really what you're doing) yourself in unhealthy ways. These are escapes that keep you from living life fully – shopping, running, alcohol, drugs, playing computer games, eating, etc. Most of those activities in and of themselves are not harmful if done in moderation. What I'm referring to here is excessiveness in any one or combination that takes you out of life and fills your hours in unproductive and potentially debilitating ways.

The second road a "do-er" may go down is one of worthwhile activities. Activities not particularly engaged in because you feel called to them, but because they fill the hours of your day. These are harder to identify because you appear to be a giving, sacrificial soul. Who can criticize you for that, right? But if your days are completely full running here and there to collect donations, chair committees, fundraise, etc., and at the end of most days you feel exhausted and depleted, ask yourself if you're running to escape real connection with people (or out of guilt, but that's a whole other subject).

Please don't hear me as saying these contributions are not valuable and worth pursuing. Yes, if you are committed to a project or organization you will feel exhausted and depleted occasionally. That's normal. But when you feel that way most days, you may want to step back and look at your true motive. Is there something you're trying to avoid and is this the method you're using?

Your rationale for not connecting with others may be, "I'm an introvert. I'm not one of those touchy-feely people that have to be around others to be happy. I'm happy alone." Please allow me to respond to that as a fellow introvert.

Let me establish that when my husband, Mike, first referred to me as an introvert, I was extremely offended and defensive. It sounded like an insult. My understanding of an introvert was a shy, timid, bookworm who sat in her room all day scared to come out and be with people. That's not me. I love people. I create retreats for women to encourage connection and empower them into living amazing lives. I regularly lead groups and facilitate discussions. I love a good party as much as the next girl; and I'm not a bad dancer if I do say so myself. So who was he to slap this pathetic label on me?

In a quick and desperate effort to redeem himself, Mike explained an introvert not as a fearful recluse or any of the other negative labels I had attached. His view is when it comes time to recharge and regenerate, introverts do it better on their own while extroverts are energized by being with people.

I don't know if that definition explains its full scope, but I like it. It fits. I love being with people, especially on our women's retreats. Yet I notice after nine days of being fully present and in deep connectedness, I desperately need alone time. My soul demands quiet time where, instead of talking or being with others, I can instead read, listen to music, pamper myself to a massage, or take a long walk. Quiet solitude is my respite.

So, if you consider yourself an introvert, maybe you simply need to recharge on your own occasionally and not use it as an excuse to separate yourself from others. Most likely there is a deeper pain preventing you from being vulnerable and connecting in a healthy way with others.

I invite you to take a minute to ask yourself the following questions:

- Is there a pain or lingering hurt I'm holding onto from the past that prevents me from truly connecting with others?

- If so, is there any part of that I can release?

- Is there anything positive I can take away from that experience?

Explore a couple ways you can still protect your heart and take baby steps to feel connection with others. I suggest starting with someone you feel safe with and then moving on to others. What would it look like if you were able to have a more meaningful conversation than simply talking about the weather or how someone's family is doing? You don't have to take this on all at once and start spewing your deep, dark secrets. You'll probably freak that person out and you won't have to worry about connecting with them. They'll be looking for their own "unfriend" button!

Trust yourself. You'll know how much is appropriate to share with the person who has earned the right to hold more of you than you've shared in the past. You'll be surprised that, even though uncomfortable at first, it will begin to feel natural with practice. Are you ready to experience relationships that ascend to a higher level and usher in joy, peace, and connectedness?

Aside from your relationship with others, do you ever feel a disconnect with yourself? These times for me can best be described as feeling a bit "off." I'm not sure what's going on and; it's not easy to put my finger on it. I feel like I've wandered off my path in life and am just going through the motions. I usually recognize this pattern after a few days when my mood has descended to feeling discouraged or down in the dumps. Once I recognize this familiar pattern of my soul needing to be nurtured, I look inward at ways to provide nurturing for myself.

It's easy to look outward for someone to fill this place for us, when no one can do it but ourselves. What works for me, and you will have your own process, is just to ask, "What do I need right now?"

Whatever process brings me back to myself is what I do. It varies from time to time. By asking myself this one simple question, I find this practice works every time for me. I'm not saying I don't wallow or feel sorry for myself from time to time. I do. I allow myself to feel those feelings fully, usually for a specific amount of time – a couple hours, a day, a week – depending on the situation. Then I gently lead myself back into self-connection.

Self-connection is probably not the most accurate word; but for me, it is restoring that connection with my Maker and my Source. When I separate myself from the One that created me, I feel a void and emptiness in all aspects of my life. The practices I use remind me of who I am and that there is a beautiful, perfect plan in place for my life. All I have to do is show up and be willing to participate in this plan by living the best version of myself. Let me share with you a wonderful occurrence I experienced on a recent trip.

I happened to take a wrong turn one day walking my Camino journey in Spain which led me down a road that would significantly alter my perception of connectedness. I found myself gazing down a lovely city walkway in Burgos, lined on either side with a unique row of trees that stretched ahead for blocks. The trees were trimmed back, a common practice with certain types of trees before the winter season. The fresh, green sprouts were beginning to burst out, and before long would surely fill the branches with lush green foliage.

On this day with most of the leaves stripped away and the bare branches exposed, I could see that several branches on every tree had fused themselves to the next, creating one continuous tree all the way down the path. Even under closer inspection, I couldn't tell where one tree ended and the next began. What an amazing and beautiful phenomenon!

Each tree appeared to be healthy, hearty, and firmly rooted. It didn't need the neighboring tree for support or to provide nutrients. I imagine it began its growth deep down in the soil, becoming solidly grounded receiving everything it needed to thrive on its own from the earth. As it became strong and healthy, its branches reached out to the next tree and they fused together. Now as one, they were infinitely stronger and able to withstand any storm together.

I questioned how it was that nature is so much wiser than we are. The trees carry out this process instinctively. We, on the other hand, often reach out when we're not firmly rooted, desperately trying to glean something from others, hoping they can fill a need we feel within ourselves. Uncomfortable with an emptiness we don't know how to fix, we look to someone else to fill that void. Sometimes the opposite occurs. We're so afraid of someone taking something (whatever that "thing" is) from us that we simply don't reach out and avoid connecting altogether.

What if we took a lesson from these trees? What if we started by securing ourselves firmly in a solid foundation, knowing we have access to everything we need; and we are whole and complete right now? I believe we'd soon realize that we don't *need* anything from anyone else to be okay. Once that knowing was solid within us, we would feel safe enough to reach out to others with no requirements to fill and not afraid that connection would deplete our own self.

What if we could reach out and connect simply to stand with each other in support and encouragement -- to love and be loved? What if?

❧ *Today's Step* ❧

Call someone you've been meaning to connect with for a while and would love to see. Invite them to lunch, coffee, happy hour, whatever works for the two of you. But here's the tricky part -- you must make it happen within five days! Put an end to the tired cliché, "Let's do lunch" when you really don't mean it. Be authentic. Laugh. Connect.

JoAnn Shares Her Story

"Walking is my connection. I've always liked to walk. As a kid I would hike in the woods surrounding our house in upstate New York. When I would tell my Mom I was headed out to explore with a PB&J sandwich and canteen filled with "goofy grape" Kool-Aid, she'd always say, 'Just be home in time for supper!'

In my teens, my best friend and I walked EVERYWHERE -- to go shopping, to concerts, to part-time jobs, and sometimes to even meet boys. (Happily, one of those boys is now my husband.) Yet at 16, I couldn't wait to get my driver's license and the freedom I believed it held....

A few years later I went to school in New York City. A great big, walkable city, and as a "New Yorker" that is how you naturally got around. Again I would head out to explore a different world on my own two feet. This is when I started to unconsciously learn that this was freedom. I could go in any direction – the wrong way down a one way street, turn right instead of left, go up instead of down, and open that door to see what was really behind it.

On foot I am connected to my world. Everything becomes clearer, multi-dimensional so to speak. I am not living my life as an outsider looking through a pane of glass. I can feel the breeze, hear it play in the trees, smell what the day might hold. I become a part of nature.

At three miles per hour, it is the human pace, the natural rhythm that we share all around the world. When walking, whether in your own neighborhood or in a faraway village (that might seem foreign), it is a way to connect to a place and its people. A nod, a wave, a smile, an invitation to share a cup of tea. It is where those serendipitous encounters lie. Though maybe only for a moment in time, a cultural connection becomes a part of who I am.

It is also a connection within myself. As you walk, your entire body is in sync. Your arms match the movement of your legs and your breathing matches your pace. It becomes a time that thoughts are free. Creative ideas emerge, problems are solved, bad moods are turned to happy, presentations are practiced. Or if need be, I can just meditate and think of... nothing."

For more information on JoAnn's walking retreats, or to comment or share your own story with her, please visit *www.ThePathThatBeckons.com*.

Chapter 8

The Path of Optimal Health

"Behandle Deinen Korper so dass
Deinen Seele Lust hat darin zu wohnen."
— Teresa von Avila

English translation:
"Treat your body such that your soul has the
desire to live within it."
— St. Teresa from Avila

Recently I was blessed to visit for a few minutes with a friend before she went into surgery to remove her breast and several lymph nodes that were ravaged by cancer. My intention was to offer support, love, positive energy, and wishes for a successful procedure and swift joyful recovery. As so often is the case in these types of situations, I found myself being the one receiving the comfort.

Becky's time with this unwelcome guest, her several rounds of chemo, and all that goes along with this process, has been such an inspiration not just to me, but everyone she comes in contact with.

She is filled with a knowing that all is well and she truly grasps the big picture. I'm sure she experiences her share of the expected emotions: anger, resentment, fear, self-pity. But she keeps coming back to that place of solace in her soul that radiates peace to all she is in contact with in her life.

One of the typical questions asked by the pre-op nurse as I sat there with her prior to surgery, was her birthdate. I knew our birthdays were close, but I was surprised to hear that we were only one day apart, born the same year. For some reason this similarity hit me in a big way. My first thought was, *Wow! We're almost the exact same age. I could be the one lying in that bed right now.* I know that's not a rational thought because age has nothing to do with being ill and no one knows what tomorrow brings. But for some reason the birthday thing really brought it home to me as a vivid reminder of my own mortality.

Good health is a luxury we typically don't appreciate until it's no longer there. If you've experienced an issue with your lungs, you no doubt have come to appreciate the simple process of breathing. The same is true of a broken leg. When you've been immobile for a while, and then are able to walk again, it's like you've received this beautiful, amazing gift of movement.

The path that beckons you right now, regardless of what path it may be, will be enhanced beyond belief by being in optimal health. You will have more energy, enthusiasm, and mental clarity to move forward. By good health, I'm not referring to a rigid diet and strenuous exercise plan. Good health, to me, is being conscious of what you're putting into your body and making the best choices at any given moment. It's keeping your body moving and maintaining your joints and muscles. This is easily achieved by walking, riding a bike, daily stretches, or practicing Yoga or Tai Chi. Exercise doesn't need to be a chore. Regard it as a gift you give yourself to maintain optimum health.

I certainly haven't been one to take the best care of my own body. In my teens I was thin and active. My twenties brought three children; and I was still thin and active. I took an aerobics class five days a week, not particularly for health reasons. I think it was more of a daily hour for myself to relax, breathe, regroup, and to be a better mother to my three little ones.

Then my thirties hit. The kids were all in school, I was working in an office, and not exercising much. As I approached my forties, I became more sedentary and experienced personal struggles. It was the first time I found myself eating for comfort. Actually, I didn't recognize it for what it was until a few years and fifty pounds later.

Have you ever had that moment when you think everything is going along normally and you catch a glimpse of the back side of yourself in the mirror as you're walking out of the bathroom, and think, *What in the world?* You slowly turn back around to take a good look at yourself, and wonder, *Who IS this person? What happened?!* That was me.

Over the next ten years I tried several eating plans. I've lost the same thirty pounds at least five or six times. To this day, my weight continues to fluctuate; and it's something I'm aware of constantly. I try to put it into perspective and not get obsessed about the number the scale reveals on any given day. Getting older, I've come to the realization that keeping excess weight off allows me to be healthy and, hopefully, around for a few years longer to spend time with my children and grandchildren, and not simply to look better in jeans. The looking better is a definite benefit, but not my driving force to be healthy and trim.

I share all this about myself because I believe many people can relate to this challenge. This is not a book about weight loss: it is a book about living your best life. I believe that coming to terms with your body shape and size, whatever that is, is a key component to living a life you love.

I've recently become aware how much my physicality affects my spirituality, even though I like to think I'm more evolved than that. I believe the saying "We're not human beings having a spiritual experience, we're spiritual beings having a human experience." But I have tell you, when I feel ill or have pain somewhere in my body, my spiritual side flies out the window (so to speak). I become very human, thinking of nothing but the discomfort and how to make it subside. I don't want to talk to anyone, and more importantly, I don't want anyone to talk to me! I am preoccupied with myself, I find it hard to be open to anything "spiritual."

In my initial attempt at hiking the Spain Camino in 2013, I broke my heel. All I could think about was getting back into my own bed, in my own home, in my own country... fast. A very sweet gentleman drove me ten miles in his taxi to the next town where I would catch a five hour bus ride to get on a plane in Madrid to take me home. The area he drove through was mountainous, lush, and absolutely stunning. He kept pointing things out to me, asking in his broken English if I'd like him to stop so I could take a picture. Over and over I replied, "No, it's fine." I had no desire whatsoever to look at this spectacular scenery. In fact, the only thing that would have made me happier would have been for him to stop talking altogether. I know that's not nice. I'm not proud of myself for thinking that way. I'm just saying, when I'm in pain I find that my world gets very small; and it's all about me. I'd like to get better at dealing with that type of situation. But for now I recognize I am much more able to walk my true path and do the most good for myself and those around me when I'm feeling healthy, physically, emotionally, and spiritually.

I am in awe of people who deal with chronic pain or conditions that limit them on a daily basis, especially those people who seem to manage that lifestyle with grace.

Most of what I've addressed concerning opti- mum health so far is focused on the physical being, but my soul craves exercise, too. I've mentioned it before because it's a practice I love. But for me jour- naling is the way I tone my emotional and spiritual muscles. Writing helps me tune into what's on my heart, reveal the next path ahead, and provide the way to take the first step. This process can also be achieved through meditation and contemplation. My daily devotional, which I read and ponder each morning, is also a key factor. It reminds me of my connection to my Creator and my unique role in this gigantic universe.

What's one gift you can give yourself today that will optimize your health? Physically? Emotionally? Spiritually? Here are some suggestions to consider:

Physically: At some point in the day, take ten minutes for movement. Walk, ride a bike, stretch, dance, twist, bend – whatever. Just move in some form. It's only ten minutes. Surely, you can fit that in.

Emotionally: As you find yourself in the midst of being busy today, stop and ask yourself, "Does this bring me joy? How can I make this easier, more fun, and less stressful?"

Spiritually: Sit quietly for a few minutes and ask yourself, "What do I really want right now?" Not for a month, a year, or the rest of your life. Just for right now.

What path is being shown before you right now? What step can you take to move closer to that path?

ᴥ Today's Step ᴥ

Look at yourself in the mirror. Really look. Now name five things you like – no, LOVE about your physical body. Next think of five things you love about yourself emotionally. Are you patient, a good listener, ambitious? And lastly, name five things you love about your soul, or who you are at your core. If this doesn't put a little spring in your step, your spring is sprung!

Terri Shares Her Story

"I was always aware of my weight, even as a child. I look back at pictures of myself growing up. I don't look any different from the other kids in my class; but I remember being told I was 'big boned' and if I didn't quit eating so many sweets I was going to end up fat like the neighbor. This neighbor lived down the road from us and was extremely overweight. I also remember being teased in elementary school about my weight. I never obsessed about it or tried losing weight until I was in high school; but it still left a lasting and negative impression on me.

I continued gaining weight, especially during my pregnancies, and never lost it after the births of my three babies. I just kept adding pounds. It didn't help that I was extremely inactive during this time.

At 300 pounds, I dealt with high blood pressure, high cholesterol, and then was diagnosed with type 2 diabetes. I didn't make any changes in my eating or exercise habits, thinking the medication I was prescribed would take care of everything. I tried every known diet, fad diet, or whatever else I thought might help me lose weight. I can't remember how many times I joined Weight Watchers. I eventually got where I wouldn't tell anyone I was on yet another quest to lose weight, because I didn't want to see the doubt and disappointment in their eyes. I even underwent lap band weight loss surgery thinking that would magically solve everything. I thought that choice would be the magic bullet. I wouldn't have to do anything and the weight would just fall off. NOT!!! I only lost 24 pounds.

The Path That Beckons

Then on January, 5th, 2009, something literally clicked in my brain. I realized I was running out of time to make positive changes with my health. I dusted off my running shoes, bought a bodybugg® to track my progress, and climbed onto the treadmill my parents had given me years earlier which until then had only been gathering dust and clothing. At first, I was only able to walk a few minutes at a time. I would have to get off, catch my breath, and then get back on for another few minutes, repeating this cycle until I had walked for twenty minutes. Finally, I was able to walk for thirty minutes at a time without feeling like I was going to die, eventually increasing my speed and lasting for up to an hour. I also started parking as far away from any of my destinations, just to get extra exercise. I overhauled how and what I ate. I learned to love vegetables, make healthy recipes, realizing I ate out of sheer boredom and laziness, not true hunger. I collected motivational quotes and posted them around my home. One of my favorites is, 'Losing weight is hard. Maintaining weight is hard. Staying fat is hard. Choose your hard.'

I still have those moments when I overeat, but I have come to the realization I need to forgive myself and get right back on the horse, so to speak.

Exercise became a huge part of my life. I loved the way it made me feel and I would almost have a panic attack if I thought I was going to miss my hour of exercise. I would even do it at 11:00 at night just to achieve my goal for the day. I told my sweet husband I would go anywhere with him as long as I had access to a gym. I knew I would have to make this a lifelong practice if I was to maintain my weight loss. I resented anything that interfered with 'my' time. It was a great way to clear my head, think through problems, and gain insights. I love the solitude it provided and the way it renewed my spirit.

On March 15th, 2010, I climbed on my scale and realized I had lost 160 pounds. A few days later, I was in the mall when I passed two women. We were the only three in that area, and one looked at me telling her friend 'There is such a thing as being too thin.' I wanted to hit her and ask, 'Do you have any idea what I have just gone through?' I have had people make fun of me and say ugly things because I was fat and now I was having the same issue with being thin! It was crazy to realize that no matter what I do someone is going to criticize and judge me.

It was fun running into people I hadn't seen in a long time and having them not recognize me. One even thought my husband had remarried!

Our son, Skyler, was also carrying around a lot of extra weight. After I reached my goal weight, he bought a treadmill and ended up losing 100 pounds, telling me I was his motivation. Two thousand and twelve ended up being a year of huge transition and change for him. Skyler separated from his wife and moved in with us for five months as he prepared to start a new job and a new life. He started running to deal with the turmoil in his life. He set his sights on running a marathon, drawing out in the lottery for the St. George, Utah marathon, to be held in October, 2012.

During the short time he lived with us that summer, together he would run and I would walk. We went approximately 6 ¾ miles round trip almost every day. It was so much fun spending this time with him. I started running only because I was afraid I was going to make him late for work. Two of Skyler's dreams were to run the St. George marathon in 10 consecutive years, being inducted into the 10 Year Club, and to qualify for the Boston marathon. So after his first marathon he bugged me to run the next one with him, to which I told him, 'I will NEVER run a marathon.' But when the time came to register for the 2013 St. George marathon, I thought Why not? Since it's a lottery, I have a 50/50 chance of **not** drawing out. Skyler called me a few weeks later, excited that we both made the cut and we were now running a marathon together. Me, at 55, the same age as the speed limit signs we would be passing during the race. What had I gotten myself into?

That was one of the best experiences of my life because I was able to run the whole marathon with Skyler. He stayed by my side while I experienced severe leg cramps for 9 of the 26.2 miles. He asked me, 'Which is worse, leg cramps or labor pains?' Also, during that time he encouraged me with, 'How many people can say they ran a marathon with their mom?' And, 'Mom, we're making memories. Those are the only things we take with us when we die.' As we crossed the finish line together, we were cheered on by my sweetheart and our grandson, Skyler's 4 year old son, Max. I realized as I crossed that finish line I was capable of doing anything I set my mind to.

One of our favorite quotes about marathons was, 'I dare you to train for a marathon and not have it change your life.' It truly did.

Skyler ran the 2014 St. George marathon by himself. He encouraged me to join him again in 2015, to which I again responded, 'NEVER. I will come and support you, but I will never run another marathon.' But once again, as I thought about it, I changed my mind and planned on telling him when he and Max came to visit us on the weekend of February 20th.

As I was getting ready for work that Friday morning, I was anticipating his reaction when I told him I had changed my mind. Approximately 30 minutes later we received the call that his 6 year old son had found him unresponsive on the floor. Max called his grandma, stating, 'I can't wake my daddy up. I think he's dead.'

On February 14th, Skyler had been running, training for the marathon. He had recently switched jobs, working a 3 p.m. to 3 a.m. shift; and had custody of his son. He had gained some weight while dealing with life as a single parent and working this crazy shift. After he finished his run and got out of the shower, he experienced severe chest pain which caused him to pass out. After he revived, he drove himself to the ER and was told he had pleuritic chest pain, that his heart and lungs were severely swollen. He was given a shot for the swelling, sent home with the instructions to walk, don't run, take Ibuprofen, and rest. All week he complained of chest pain, especially when he tried to rest. He died the morning of February 20th, 2015 from aortic dissection, fluid between his heart and the myocardial sac.

How does a parent even begin to say goodbye to their child? It's your worst nightmare; and 30 years wasn't nearly long enough to spend with our amazing son.

After Skyler died I found myself eating all kinds of junk food and in large amounts. I didn't seem to be able to stop. I wondered what was wrong with me. A friend at work told me how his brother turned to alcohol when his son died. I thought about this for most of that day thinking, That's a stupid way to deal with grief, using drugs or alcohol to numb the pain. It changes absolutely nothing, won't bring them back, and only creates more problems. I felt like someone hit me in the back of the head

as I realized I was doing exactly the same thing; but I had
been using food as my drug of choice, trying to numb my
own pain and grief. I had to once again forgive myself and
get back on track. Skyler wouldn't want me to gain weight
because of his death. Luckily, I hadn't stopped walking
during this time.

Our sweet son had a huge, loving heart and a big
smile. He blessed others with his happy, positive outlook
on life, even when he was lonely, sad, or hurting. He could
make any experience or adventure fun. He had a way of
drawing people to him.

I was blessed to be along for the whole amazing,
frustrating, and sometimes crazy, but mostly wonderful
experience of being his mom. From witnessing his first
tentative steps to the 'I don't want that bowl, too much milk,
not enough milk, wanting the milk out of the new container
not the old one, the wrong kind of cereal, too much cereal,
not enough cereal, or it was the wrong spoon' days. Or when
he'd have the neighborhood kids lined up on the front lawn
playing dead bodies (his dad is a funeral director).

There was never a dull moment when Skyler was
around. When he was little, he found a rubber ball which
had been cut and turned inside out. He wore it like a hat,
with the valve stem on the top of his head. He called it his
stinger hat.

He and his friends would float down the nearby creek
every summer on inner tubes. One summer I witnessed
Skyler with a car full of his friends, his very large, lime
green inflatable arm chair tied to the top of the car, headed
once again to float down the creek, and me thinking,
That's my Skyler.

I watched him become a new father and a wonderful
daddy to Max, who was his whole life. This son of ours

taught us to never judge a person – just love them. After he died I had several individuals reach out to me in private messages, people I have never met and will probably never meet, sharing their stories of how Skyler had given them a chance when they were down, out, and truly desperate, and how that chance changed their lives.

I watched him encourage two young runners at the St. George marathon and then honor the 9 year old boy when he and his father stopped into the restaurant on their way home the next day. After Skyler finished congratulating him, the patrons applauded his accomplishment and Skyler bought his lunch. That boy will always remember Skyler, even if he never knew his name. The motto Skyler lived his life by was: 'Your smile is your logo, your personality is your business card. How you leave others feeling after having an experience with you becomes your trademark.'

Skyler was my running buddy, my inspiration, my sunshine, and my heart. He and I ran three 5ks, two 10ks, three half marathons, and, of course, the full marathon in 2013. I honestly didn't think I could run another marathon, especially so soon after his death. But as I thought about it, I decided this was a way I could honor his memory: his love for and desire to run ten consecutive St. George Marathons.

I registered for the marathon and once again thought, I have a 50/50 chance of **not** drawing out in the lottery. But on May 7, 2015, I received notification I made it.

It will be an extremely emotional day for me, very hard knowing that I won't be running it with him, but for him. I'm sure there will be days when I don't know if I can run that marathon, but there will be a lifetime knowing that I did it for Skyler."

Note: Along with her niece, Terri ran and completed the St. George Marathon in October 2015 in honor of her son, Skyler!

If you'd like to comment or share your own story with Terri, please visit *www.ThePathThatBeckons.com.*

Chapter 9

The Path of Love

"Love isn't the most important thing,
it's the ONLY thing."
– I.M. Lamb

On all the paths we're exploring, the core of each is love. It may take on different aspects and manifest in the form of compassion, service, a listening ear, or a warm hug, but it must be the basis of all we do. Otherwise, our efforts are in vain.

Of the numerous beautiful lessons and messages in the Bible, two are my favorite by far. Jesus was very clear when asked by a scribe which commandment was the most important. He answered, "You shall love the Lord your God with all your heart and with all your soul and with all your mind and with all your strength." Right after that, He said, "You shall love your neighbor as yourself. There is no other commandment greater than these." – Mark 12: 30-31.

First, love your Maker, your Creator, with all you have. Second, love your neighbor (not just those who live by you!), but all people on the planet. And third, love yourself. The third part seems to get downplayed sometimes. But I believe in order to fully love others, we must first love ourselves.

So, let's start with the third person mentioned in this verse – you.

Are you one of those people who find it easy to forgive and accept others, but can't seem to extend that same grace and compassion to yourself? Don't feel alone. It's easy to replay those old memories of the times we came up short, acted inappropriately, or did or said things we desperately wish we could take back. Those videos in our heads are usually as crisp and clear as if they happened yesterday; while it can be more difficult to recall times when we've stepped up to the occasion, extended a hand to someone who desperately needed it, or performed an unexpected act of kindness.

If this is a struggle for you, I invite you to take a few minutes right now and do the following exercise.

- Make a list of three things you've done, either recently or in the past, that elicit good feelings from yourself and allow you to love who you were being in that instance.

- Go back to that moment in time and really experience how you felt when you did those things.

- Did you bring a much needed smile to someone's face? Did you surprise someone? Did you hold a space for someone to pour out their heart to you where you didn't offer a solution, but just listened?

- Experience a renewed appreciation for yourself and rejoice in who you are.

Now let's make a second list.

- Write down three times that weren't your most shining moments.

- Identify times where you were disappointed in yourself by something you said or did. Be honest. No one is going to read this except you.

- As you compile the list, notice the feelings that arise, but try not to let shame or other negative feelings take hold. You're listing these events objectively, as an outsider looking on without judgment.

- When finished with the list, (Stop at three; we don't want to go down a crazy dark road here.) take a few minutes to look at them one at a time.

- Remind yourself that these are in the past. Is there an action you can take today to change any of the regrettable acts? Probably not. However, if something is still hanging out there feeling unfinished, you may want to consider how to put this to rest forever. Do you need to apologize to someone? Or maybe just forgive yourself?

- Look at the person you were at the time this event occurred. Do you recognize why you did or said what you did? This is not justifying it or making it right; it's simply owning your humanness and extending love and grace to yourself as a person who makes mistakes and uses them to learn and grow.

Now, the big question: Can you love yourself, not in spite of this offense, but *along with* this offense? It's part of your history and part of you. You can choose to ignore it or beat yourself up over it, or you can let it go and love yourself. It's up to you.

It may take a little time, but use this process for each item on your list. Release yourself from guilt or shame. They don't serve you, and they don't serve anyone else either. It's hard to truly love your life when you're harboring animosity toward yourself.

Now, let's move on to the second person mentioned in the verse – your neighbor.

Creating a spirit of love towards others in all you do can be trying at times. If people would just "act right" they'd be a lot easier to love, right? Or to put it another way, if everyone would just do what I want, they'd be easier to love. But they don't. People mess up. They disappoint. They irritate the crap out of you.

When you can practice loving them, even in those situations, your idea and experience of love will totally be transformed.

Next, make a new list. Following the same steps as you did in the process for yourself, write down any ill feelings you hold against another person. This will be one of the most freeing exercises you will experience. You're not saying what they did was okay, or condoning their actions. You are simply releasing the hold they have over you which in turn prevents you from fully loving others.

Then list five qualities you love about that person and how your life has been blessed by them. In some instances, the only positive thing you may find about them is the lesson they taught you; and that lesson could be to empower you to unhook the hold someone else's action has over you. Sometimes people who are the hardest to be around provide the most valuable lessons.

Going through this process for yourself and for others will allow you to be free to love in, and in spite of, all situations, if you let it. What a precious gift you have just given yourself.

Unfortunately, this process is not one that can be done once and then it's over. It's something that needs to be repeated again and again. Maybe once a week or once a month, check in with yourself and ask, "Is there anyone or anything preventing me from fully expressing unconditional love in my life?" As you become more loving in your daily actions, you'll notice sooner when there is something blocking that flow. The quicker you can identify it and release it, the less time you lose in that negativity funk.

Let's say you've taken some time to thoughtfully go through this process for yourself and for others. You feel renewed, light and overflowing with love. Now what?

Now is when you get to be creative in how to demonstrate this exhilaration. This is where your personality shines through. Do what you love to do. Your unique way of expressing love may look like compassion. You may want to volunteer or take dinner to a neighbor who's been ill. It may show up as service where you babysit to give a young mom a few hours to herself, or maybe you raise money for a cause that's important to you. Your version of love may appear in the form of humor. Maybe you take a friend who's struggling, out to lunch to cheer them up, or retell a joke you just heard. Sharing your unique personality, talents, and gifts is you sending out ripples of love in many aspects of life. Your life will be better for it and the lives of others richly blessed. You never know; the smile you offer someone in the supermarket may be the only one they get all day. So even though you may not see the rewards of your efforts, you can trust it IS making a difference in your life, the lives of others, and the world.

Today's Step

Give yourself a gift – a gift of love. Only you know what that looks like. And then, give someone else a gift of love. Again, you get to decide. Be creative. Be sincere. I feel love in the air already. Don't you?

And, now the first person mentioned in this passage, first and foremost is to love the Lord, your God.

I don't want to impose my beliefs onto you. I share this deeply personal experience because it was extremely powerful and meaningful for me. You are free to do with it what you will.

There was a time in my life, in my late thirties, when I questioned my relationship with and existence of God. My impression of Him was a pissed off old man sitting out there somewhere on a throne, sporting a long white beard looking down on everyone with distain – especially me. I felt I was a disappointment and someone He wasn't very happy with. So I decided I didn't like Him very much either; and I certainly didn't need that feeling of unworthiness and shame in my life. When I least expected it, everything changed.

My Personal Story

"It was Easter weekend, 2000. I flew from Arizona to Texas to spend the holiday weekend with Mike, my husband, before he was my husband. This was during the five years we were seeing each other and flying back and forth between the two states. (Not long after that, he conceded and moved to Arizona and we were married.)

It was Saturday morning. Mike had a few clients to see. Then the plan was to pick me up, spend a little time checking out the local flea market, and go to the grocery store to buy what we needed for dinner the next day. An Easter barbecue was planned for several friends who would come and enjoy the day with us.

As soon as my eyes opened that morning, a thought clearly popped into my head, *You need to go see your mom.* My mom lived in Utah, which as you know, is nowhere near south Texas; so this was a completely unexpected and bizarre idea.

My mom struggled with diabetes and had been managing the effects the disease had left on her body over the past 30 years. She was diligent. She took her insulin shots faithfully, ate exactly as she knew she needed to, and exercised often. But even with all that, the disease had progressed and taken its toll on her body. She'd had two massive heart attacks in her forties, which resulted in by-pass surgery and several complications before age 46. She continually powered through it all with relentless grace, strength, and optimism. But now it was 13 years since her by-pass surgery; and she was experiencing congestive heart failure. At this point, there was not much more the doctors could do. Even though I felt she would be around forever (Don't all kids think that about their parents?) arrangements were in place for my three children and me to fly to Utah for a visit in two weeks.

So, you see why this prompt today was confusing. I found myself rationalizing with that voice in my head, *I'll be there in two weeks. I don't need to go today. We have plans for Easter. This is my weekend to spend with Mike. Besides, Utah isn't even close.* But the voice wouldn't be silenced, *You need to go see your mom.*

I decided to call her. That would surely confirm everything was okay. We exchanged small talk. I asked her how she was feeling; and she reassured me she was fine. She said she and her husband, Roger, were going up to the cabin tomorrow for lunch by the lake. We wished each other a Happy Easter, said our I love you's and hung up. *There. See? Concerned over nothing.*

I proceeded to get ready for the day, but that relentless voice wouldn't quit. Over and over, it kept repeating the same thing, *'You need to go see your mom.'*

Mike picked me up and we headed to the flea market to see what kind of treasures we could find. By now, the voice was screaming. It was so loud, I couldn't concentrate on our conversation. Feeling frustrated and a little silly, I shared what was going on with Mike. I prefaced it with, *'I don't know why I have this feeling. I'm going to see her in two weeks. I spoke with her this morning and she sounds fine.'* I will never forget his insightful response. *'It doesn't matter WHY this is happening. You just need to do it. Don't question it. Let's change your flight. I'll drive you to San Antonio today; and you'll be there tomorrow.'* (San Antonio was a 3 ½ hour drive away.)

I called and rearranged my flight, paying a hefty change fee, all the while thinking how crazy this was. I had been looking forward to spending Easter weekend with Mike; and now I was making this random flight to Utah because of some stupid voice in my head. Was I losing my mind?

Now I had to call my mom back to tell her I was coming to Utah without having her think something strange was up (which it was). I called her with a lame story about my flight back home tomorrow being rerouted through Salt Lake. So I decided to take advantage of it and come visit her for a couple days. Thankfully, my mom wasn't much of a traveler, because I think she actually bought the story. But what she said next rocked me to the core and validated this odd prompting. She said she'd rather I not come to see her. She continued by saying she really wasn't doing that well and didn't want me to see her in that condition. My heart broke and I started to silently cry. It was clear something was desperately wrong. She would never have asked me not to come see her as she counted the days between our visits.

I assured her no matter what was going on or how she looked, I didn't care. She was my mom and I loved her. I told her I'd see her in the morning.

My disbelief and doubt shifted to concern and then fear. I flew into Salt Lake City the next morning and drove the long two hour drive to Price, the small town where I spent the first 28 years of my life. I pulled up at my brother's house where Roger's truck was in the driveway, idling. He was in the house taking an Easter treat to my niece while my mom sat waiting in the truck – something completely out of character for her. I pulled up, walked over to the passenger side of the truck, and opened the door. I did my best to hide the shock and sadness that washed over me as I looked into those eyes that had always been such bright blue, but now were cloudy. A frail, thin sickly woman sat in the spot my energetic, bubbly mom usually occupied. I wanted to embrace her and make everything better; but I knew I couldn't make it better.

The next couple days provided some of the most poignant, precious memories I have of my beautiful mother. We lay on the bed together when she was too exhausted to do anything. We went out to her favorite restaurant where she did her best to eat less than a quarter of a sandwich. I drove the car up to the restaurant door because she was too weak to walk to the parking lot. It was on the back steps enjoying the warm sunshine where she told me how much she wanted me to be happy, and that she hoped Mike was a man that would take care of me and love me. I assured her he was up for the job.

The last night before I left, I witnessed what is one of my most cherished memories and example of true love. Because she was retaining so much water, my mom's feet were extremely swollen, so that she could barely walk. Sitting in the living room, I felt like an intruder witnessing an intimate moment meant for just the two of them. I watched as Roger sat on the floor in front of her tenderly massaging her feet to ease her discomfort. It was so symbolic of their relationship. He had stepped into her life at a time she really needed him. He had been there to ease her pain and make her life happy. They were like teenagers, her sitting next to him in the truck and the two holding hands every chance they had. I knew Roger was fully aware he would be losing his best friend and the love of his life soon. I wondered how he would deal with it when that heartbreaking day arrived.

The next morning we said good bye and I headed back to Salt Lake to fly home. Before leaving, I assured her that I'd be back in ten days with the kids. I had a sense she didn't believe it was going to happen; but it was just ten days. Yes. It would. It would happen.

Seven days later, my mom was hospitalized. She stayed for observation for a couple days and was set to be discharged Friday morning, which was the same day I was arriving with my children to see their beloved Grandma. This would surely put a smile on her face.

Friday morning, just before my alarm went off, I got the call no one wants to receive. It was my brother saying my mom had passed away that morning.

I've replayed that whole experience many times in my mind. Each time I am absolutely amazed by the sacred unfolding of each step. This precious gift was just that – a gift I will cherish my entire life. From that moment forward, the way I viewed my God was completely different. That cranky old man image has been replaced by absolute pure love. I know beyond a shadow of a doubt that I am loved so much more than I can comprehend. This is not something I imagined or made happen on my own. In fact, I fought it as long as I could. But this Person, this Source, this Powerful Force I call my Father in Heaven, knew how much I loved my mom, and perfectly orchestrated a plan for us to share one last precious time together while on this earth. As a recipient of that pure sweet love, I am eternally grateful."

If you'd like to comment or share your own story with me, Debbie, please visit *www.ThePathThatBeckons.com*.

Part 4

Embracing Your Journey

Chapter 10

The Path of Passion

"Passion is your joy. It is the essence of who you are.
You have to unwrap it and find it."
– Jackie St. Onge

Have you ever felt like something's not quite right, but you're not sure what is off? Things appear to be going okay, but there's something you just can't put your finger on that is missing from your life.

There was a period of time (more than one really, but one that was monumental) when I felt that way. My kids were doing well. My career was going okay, not great, but okay. My marriage was how I expected most long-term unions were – no real problems, but not fantastic.

So, what was this void I was experiencing?

Then it hit me – I had nothing in my life that I was really passionate about. As I opened my eyes in the morning, nothing caused me to leap out of bed eagerly anticipating the new day. I had fallen into a rut and wanted to reclaim that fire I felt in the past.

I sat down with my pen and legal pad (surprise, surprise.) and began to brainstorm. What do I love to do? What fills me with enthusiasm? How can I reignite my passion?

I knew it couldn't be anything really wild. After all, I did have a family to tend to, a home to maintain, and a career. My daily routine was already pretty time-consuming. What I needed was an occasional spark to regenerate and enliven me.

I compiled a list of things I loved to do, but hadn't done in a while. The first on my list was going to the movies. I don't know how or when this simple activity had disappeared from my life, but I'm guessing the introduction of video rentals was the culprit. I couldn't recall the last time I'd been out to a movie, probably years.

This may sound like a simple thing, but I immediately got excited about the prospect of actually watching a movie in a real theater. I remembered how much I loved silly romantic classics, indie films, and movies that were a bit "off the wall." It's not always easy to find people who enjoy those genres, so if I did go see a movie, it wasn't usually one of these types. I was ready to reintroduce some quirky, fun movie-going entertainment into my life!

I devised a plan for an adventure that was a huge stretch for me at the time. I would go to a movie. During the day. Alone.

I'd never been to movie solo, so this was way outside my comfort zone. I chose to go during the day when the theater wouldn't have many people to take pity on me assuming I didn't have any friends to go with me. I summoned up my courage and drove myself to the theater, all the while questioning my decision. While I felt a bit crazy for doing this, I did it. Quieting the need to explain my unaccompanied appearance, I purchased a ticket for one. I entered the lobby where I treated myself to a soda and popcorn, and turned to enter the dark theater. Relieved, I counted only five other fellow movie-goers, and one brave soul was also going it alone.

I selected my seat on the back row and got situated. I laughed out loud when a singsong poem of my mom's ran through my head. *I love myself. I love me so. I took myself to the picture show. I put my arm around my waist, but if I get fresh, I'll slap my face.* (Don't worry, there was no funny stuff going on… in my area at least.)

It's been over twenty years now, but I remember like it was yesterday the movie playing. It was "Sabrina," the 1995 remake with Harrison Ford and Julie Ormand. Even though it's not what I would necessarily consider a classic, it transported me to another realm. I laughed. I cried. *I felt!* This was what

I had been missing: emotion, joy, sadness, laughter, love, passion!

For several months, I had a standing Wednesday afternoon date with myself which I excitedly anticipated each week. I experimented with viewing thought-provoking and emotionally charged movies and documentaries.

My teenage daughter, Stacey, was mortified at the thought of one of her friends running into her mom at the movies alone. My defense was that if they were in the movie theater on a Wednesday afternoon instead of school, they're the ones who needed to worry. Because it was during the school day, we were both safe.

It sounds so simple, and it was, but it's amazing how much of a shift resulted from this one small action. The door cracked open. I was eager to experience passion and enthusiasm in other areas of my life as well.

A second practice I implemented, once I became comfortable with being alone and not relying on someone else to make me happy, was taking myself out to lunch. (I don't have a funny poem about that.) I still continue to indulge in this guilty pleasure once or twice a month. I usually explore a restaurant or café that may not appeal to my husband's tastes and treat myself to this unique experience.

I've shared this idea with women and many can't imagine eating in a restaurant alone. If you're one of those people who balk at the idea of dining solo, I have a few tips for you.

- Go between 2 p.m. – 4 p.m. It's past the lunch rush and generally fairly quiet. You'll probably feel more comfortable when seated at a table by yourself.

- Bring a book to read or your journal to write in. It gives you something to focus on while eating, and makes you appear to be up to something productive or important!

- Tip well. If you find a place that becomes *your* place, the servers will appreciate your generosity and go out of their way to make your experience more pleasurable.

One of the unexpected outcomes of this practice for me was a new appreciation of food. Alone and not distracted by conversation, I am able to concentrate on what I put into my mouth. I try new dishes, savoring the unfamiliar flavors and textures. It's a different dining experience when you are keenly aware of the texture, the aroma, and the variety of herbs and spices in what you eat. I understand now what it means to be passionate about food.

These are two super easy examples of ways to invite a little more oomph into your life. There are a million more. Keep in mind, these are not the end result to finding passion; they are merely an opening to begin recognizing what makes you feel happy and alive and doing more of that.

Now would be a good time to check in with yourself to see if this is a path that's beckoning you right now. If so, start your list. Place the list somewhere you'll see it throughout the day. As the idea, "Wouldn't it be fun to …" pops into your head, write it down. Even if it's not the right thing right now, someday it may be. It's a fun exercise that gets the creative juices flowing and who knows what adventures it will spark or what it will lead to!

Today I'm in a different season in life. My children are grown with children of their own. I've retired from my career, and my husband and I support each other in following our individual dreams and passions, as well as creating new ones together. I'm free to explore in more diverse ways.

These days I find myself passionate about supporting and empowering women; pursuing my personal spiritual journey in ways like walking the pilgrimage Camino de Santiago; organizing and leading women's retreats; traveling to diverse countries; entertaining family and friends in our home; and hiking with my husband.

I believe it all began twenty years ago by being brave enough to start with something as simple as taking responsibility for how I felt, not placing that onus on someone else, and just taking myself out to a movie or lunch.

How will you start?

Today's Step

You know what I'm going to say, don't you? Pick a restaurant you've been dying to try, but haven't yet. Take yourself on a date. If you're feeling really adventurous, go see that movie you haven't found anyone who has expressed an interest in seeing. Move through your initial resistance and enjoy your own company. (If you need to, you can borrow my little song.) You can do it!

Mackenzie Shares Her Story

"My name is Mackenzie. My hobbies are baking and having fun with my friends. I am ten years old and in 5th grade. I have a dog named Murphy and a Russian Tortoise named Emily. I love to bake cakes. I got inspired by my dad, who is a wonderful cook around the house. One of my favorite dishes he makes is his homemade Italian pasta and sauce. I usually help him with making the meatballs. The reason I like that is because we both have a passion for cooking and get to spend time together. That is the reason I wanted to start cooking instead of baking at first. But when I tried baking, I found that much easier. I liked the way I could decorate the cakes I make and the way it lets my imagination flow.

The first birthday cake I made was for my brother on his seventh birthday. It was kind of challenging because I had to make two layers. I decorated it like a video game controller because he really likes video games. I have to say, it was pretty good for my first time. My brother thought it was cool, but I think he was expecting it to be better. I felt good about myself especially for my first try.

But they don't always turn out like I expect them to. On my cousin Noah's birthday, I was making the cake at home. When the timer went off, I tested the cake and thought it was done. So I took it out. When it was cool I took it out of the pan, and it was raw! So we had to go get more ingredients and make the cake again. After I decorated it like Pokemon, we finally got to the party. Noah said it looked 'Awesome', and we ate the cake.

So, now I bake birthday cakes for my family members such as my cousins, grandpa, my brother, and my uncle. Part of the fun is decorating them and seeing how excited everyone gets when their birthdays are coming up.

A few more I have made are a My Little Pony cake, an Iron Man cake, and a Black Jack cake. So far I have made eight birthday cakes; but there are more that I have made that are not birthday cakes.

I love to see the expression on my family's face when I walk in the door with the cake. My favorite part of making the cakes is decorating them. I try to show the personality of the person who gets the cake by decorating with what they like. The cakes I make are unique and a special present for them especially made by me.

If you would like to try baking I think you can do it at any age; because I am only ten and have made about twelve cakes for my family. Start off easy. Then when you think you can move on to more challenging things, go ahead and do so. I know you can accomplish anything."

If you'd like to comment or share your own story with Mackenzie, through her parents, please visit *www.ThePathThatBeckons.com*.

Chapter 11

The Path of Infinite Possibilities

"Most of the time you don't know how close a dream is to coming true, until after it has."
– Mike Dooley

Many times we ask for a situation or condition in our lives to change, or for a transformation within elevating us to a higher level of being. These commendable and courageous intentions don't always transpire easily. After all, you are asking for *transformation!* That's not a little improvement – that's a leap. So, be ready.

Last year, I experienced a transformation involving more than one transition simultaneously. The first was to sell my business that had provided financial support for my family for twenty years. The second was to step back and re-evaluate my participation in a venture I was involved in with my two sisters for the past five years. Both were major changes on several levels – financial, personal, and emotional, to name a few.

The decision was made and the wheels put into motion to make these intentions realities. They both transpired so quickly and smoothly I was caught off guard, not fully prepared for the end result. I expected the process to take several months to come to fruition. Was I ever in for a surprise! I didn't find a buyer for my business. A complete stranger, with whom I was making small talk at a restaurant as we were both waiting for other people to join us, offered to buy my business. The owner agreed readily to the asking price; and within 60 days the entire process was signed and sealed. It was nothing less than a miracle. Every step fell into place perfectly. This was amazing and unusual, at least for me. My transitions in the past seemed to have been more involved, complex, and, yes, even painful. I am finding when you allow yourself to be open to synchronicity and ease, and let go of the drama, amazing things happen in your life.

I was elated as this process went off without a hitch, yet I felt a door close behind me, both figuratively and literally.

When I shared my feelings about altering my involvement in the business venture with my sisters, they were loving and supportive. That transition was a smooth one, as well. A second door closed behind me, a little louder this time.

The next transition was the ending of a business relationship with a friend of fourteen years. The third door slammed shut.

Three doors closed behind me that would most likely never be opened again, and, even if they did, what was behind them wouldn't look the same. Three endings in my life all at once.

The best way to describe the feeling that overcame me is standing in a dark hallway with doors to my back locked and bolted, and no new doors to open ahead of me. I didn't have a plan, or even a clue, where I would go next or how to get there. It felt heavy and dark. I experienced emotions similar to when a loved one passes away. I grieved for the losses. Even though I knew it was time to move on – I wanted to move on – and I trusted there was something more amazing than I could imagine, it was hard. That's the thing about transitions. We place our focus and excitement on the new, shiny experience, and forget that space needs to be created. This typically includes letting go of something.

I stood in that hallway alone, in the not knowing, and trusted. I trusted that an answer would be shown to me. It was uncomfortable. I was tempted to do something, anything. Even though it wasn't easy, I convinced myself to be still and give up my need to "fix it" or make it better. My loving husband, who witnessed firsthand my struggle, was my greatest support. He encouraged me to be at peace with the silence, to rest in this lull in my life, and to be open to possibilities as they make themselves known.

I share this because I don't believe my experience is unique. I've talked with several women who are in the middle of some form of transition or transformation. When I relate the dark hallway metaphor, many resonate with feeling something similar that they haven't been able to put into words.

One consolation of my recent transformation is that it came about as a result of choices I made. It helped ease the discomfort when I reminded myself the reason I was in this situation was to grow in a new positive way in my life.

When you find yourself experiencing a transition that was not your choice, it's a different situation.

Let's say, for example, that you've been diagnosed with celiac disease and now must completely change your diet. Slam! You discover your husband has been having an affair for the past five years, and is now asking for a divorce. Slam! Your seventeen year old daughter tearfully confides she thinks she's pregnant. Slam!

You didn't ask for any of these things. Who would? But, like it or not, they are now your reality. How do you handle the transition that is about to take place in your life? Do you hide, finding solace in a few glasses of wine every chance you get? Do you put up morbid decorations for a long and maudlin pity party? Do you call your friends spewing the venom of your anger, resentment, and frustration?

I'm not saying you don't deserve to knock out a bottle of Pinot Noir, cry until you have no more tears, or throw a tantrum. You've just had the rug pulled out from under you, and are forced to face life completely different than it was yesterday.

My suggestion is that you don't stay too long in any of those places. Feel what you're feeling and express it as you need to, hopefully with the least number of witnesses present to see your tantrum. I say this in jest because someday you will get past this and people have long memories. Eventually someone in your circle will tease you about the event, saying, "Remember when you …"

There will come a day when you're sick of the pity party and hiding, and ready to move on. I know this sounds flippant; and I apologize if you're in the beginning stages of this process. But I believe in the end you will find this may be one of the best things that could have happened to you. Life has a way of taking heartbreaking experiences and creating something beautiful and wonderful from them, if you're willing to see what unfolds. In time, you may realize that what seemed horrible provided something beautiful for you or someone you love.

You may experience the same "dark hall" phenomenon; and this time you will have helplessness added to the emotions. But, there is another door for you to open. You may have to wait a bit or look really closely; but a tiny sliver of light will shine as that door is cracked ever so slightly.

So, now that we know many people experience this, what's the answer? Do you stop asking for growth in your life? Do you avoid change or progress? Of course not. What I found works for me is to recognize whatever is happening for what it is, and give up my initial reaction to fight against it or muscle through. Use this quiet season in your life, the in-between time, to nurture yourself. What would make you feel better in this moment? Would you like to take a contemplative walk? Or are you more of a "drive with the windows down in your car with rock and roll blaring on the radio" kind of person? What things have you wanted to do for a while, but haven't? Explore and be open to those ideas. Try something new. After all, you're in a transition; there are going to be lots of new things coming your way. Why not start practicing and getting comfortable with change now?

Before you know it, you'll be ready to explore what's waiting for you on what is one of my favorite paths, that of *Infinite Possibilities.*

I envision this path as a diverse way with gentle twists and unexpected turns, one with rolling hills that you can't see over until you've ventured to the top, and dips into enchanting valleys. It's lined with a variety of trees covered by bark of different colors and leaves displaying countless textures and shapes, and a myriad of foliage in a rainbow of colors. Playful birds play tag with each other from tree to tree; furry creatures frolic in the meadows. Exotic butterflies lead as you embark on this magical journey.

It may appear completely different in your mind's eye. That's the beauty of infinite possibilities: they're YOUR possibilities and they appear how YOU want.

This path allows you to play freely and at your own pace with all options available to you at this point in time. I suggest you get a notebook. (I'd say journal, but I'm sure you're getting sick of hearing that word!) Make it one with a picture or words on the cover resonating with the possibilities you're anticipating. Mine has a bright red, soft leather cover with the words, "I dwell in possibility. – Emily

Dickinson." Whenever I pick up that journal to dream, I think to myself, "Why, yes, I do!"

In your book of possibilities, dream. Dream big. Don't censure or critique your dreams or worry that someone else will see them. Just dream. Dreaming and imagining are beautiful qualities we sadly stop allowing ourselves to do as we become adults. If you lack inspiration, spend time with children. They are masters at dreaming and pretending.

Ask yourself these questions:

- If money, other people's opinion, and rational thinking were not factors in my decision, what would I really love to do?

- What are some experiences that bring me real joy?

- What ways do I bring joy to others?

- What's my natural way of being which comes effortlessly?

- What's one thing I can spend my time doing for hours and feel like no time has passed?

You don't need to have the details all figured out. You're just playing pretend for now.

The key to this process is not to allow your logical side (or as I like to call it, your Dream Killer) to have a voice in the conversation. It'll try to get your attention by saying things like, "That's a stupid idea. You can't do that. Someone's already doing it."

As often as that little gremlin keeps piping up, just remember its purpose is to keep you safe and where you are in life. So, don't fight it. Thank it for doing its job. Reassure it you're safe and can handle this situation all by yourself.

And go on making that list.

As you start this process, you'll find new ideas coming to you when you least expect it. As they do, jot them down in your Dream Book. There is a beautiful, infinite realm of possibilities awaiting – you just have to be brave enough to dream!

🐾 *Today's Step* 🐾

Is there a practice, hobby, or sport you loved as a child or young person, but you haven't thought about or practiced for years? Today, reflect and experience the feelings you had while spending time in this activity. Is there some version of this activity you can implement in your life right now that will light you up?

Take one step toward it, or whatever shows up for you today. Reignite your passion and be open to possibilities. They're infinite!

Janette's Story as Seen Through the Eyes of Her daughter, Mary Ann

"*In addition to being one of my best friends, my mom is one of the strongest, most inspiring people I know. As a widow for more than twenty years, she leads a very full life. I always say she's 79 going on 50; and I hope I'm doing even half what she does when I'm her age. Above all, I think of Mom as an artist. The funny thing is, she didn't always describe herself that way.*

Janette was born in rural Oklahoma to hard-working parents whose families both came over in the Oklahoma Land Run. Grandpa worked for Conoco, bred and raised champion quarter-horses in the '40s and '50s, and raised cattle until the day he died. Grandma was a hunting, fishing, pioneer-type woman, who did everything from being a live-in housekeeper to working at the dime store and as a telephone switchboard operator during the Depression to make a living. They instilled a great sense of family and responsibility in my mother.

Besides growing up riding horses, Mom lifeguarded in the summers, swam competitively – even making the Junior Olympics in 1950, played the piano and sang in the church choir. Through it all, she loved art, and started drawing when she was four or five.

Mom really wanted to be an artist, but the general consensus was, and maybe still is, that it's hard to make money as an artist. At least in her part of the country, women typically aspired to be housewives, unless they decided to become a secretary, nurse, or teacher. Mom attended Oklahoma State University as an Art Education major as a way to combine her love of art with teaching. Mom met my Dad, who, while they were dating, was called to serve in the Army Engineer Corps. When Dad returned from Korea, they got married, finished school, and eventually moved to Amarillo, Texas, where they raised my sister, brother, and me. Dad joined a local architecture firm and Mom taught art at a local junior high for one year. However, once my sister was born, Mom put her art/teaching career aside and concentrated on raising a family.

She did everything! She cooked, cleaned, sewed, sang in the choir, was involved in PEO and Sunday School, baked lots of cookies as a homeroom mother, and also managed to serve as Cub Scout Den Mother and Brownie and Girl Scout troop leader for us kids! Mom occasionally substituted for one of the art museum teachers, and when that teacher was moving, she recognized Mom's talent and recommended she take over. While Mom's classes included drawing and painting for all ages, including both gifted and special needs students, she didn't really pursue her own art. We had paintings and prints around the house that she'd done in college, but I can't remember seeing her paint. She was content to raise us kids and be the best mom she could, even though she always wanted to "be an artist."

As a family, we took lots of trips; and Mom and Dad had plans to travel and enjoy their retirement together. They dreamed of taking an RV and following the fall colors down from Canada through the U.S., painting as they went.

Unfortunately, they never got to pursue most of their plans, as we lost my dad to cancer at 61 – Mom was only 58. I was a senior in college and remember being terrified *she might follow in my grandmother's footsteps. You see, I remember my sweet little Grandma sort of 'settling into old age' after Grandpa died. She lived in a retirement community, visited with neighbors and friends, and reminisced about her younger days for another eleven years until she eventually passed peacefully in her sleep. Mom did give us a scare about a year after Dad died. She ended up in the hospital with a collapsed lung, but came through the experience with flying colors. Fortunately, it seems I had nothing to fear. Twenty-one years later, Mom is still inspiring me with her strength, her adventurous spirit, and her sense of humor. We joke that she has a bionic leg, due to a misstep that ended with surgery to insert a titanium rod in her leg. She also is a breast cancer survivor. I'd say Mom definitely knows how to overcome challenges!*

There was a point at which Mom learned to create the life she wanted. In the mid-90s, not long after Dad passed, Mom, my sister, and I all separately attended a personal development seminar that would change our views of ourselves and our 'stories,' particularly our limiting beliefs. Through that workshop, Mom chose to stop saying, 'I want to be an artist' and shifted it to, 'I am an artist!' She took a pastel workshop a few years later and ended up entering shows at the Panhandle Art Center. Since then, Mom has traveled the world producing numerous works of art: pastels, watercolors, oils, landscapes, abstracts, etc. She's returned to Europe several times with friends and other artists, and has been to Scotland, England, Ireland, Italy, France, and Russia.

Besides her international travel, she's painted all over the U.S., from Cape Cod to various parts of the Southwest. One of my favorite pieces is a watercolor she painted of Cathedral Rock in Sedona, from a trip she and I took to Jazz on the Rocks for Mother's Day. She gave it to my husband and me as a wedding gift.

We've lost count of how many paintings she's sold. They range from landscapes, based on pictures she's taken around the world, to works she's been commissioned to do. She's had paintings purchased by the Dumas, Texas Art Museum, the Carson County Art Museum in New Mexico, and the Texas Tech University Laura Bush Women's Health Sciences Center for their permanent collections. She's won awards from the Lone Star Pastel Society and the Southeast Colorado Art Guild. She still teaches occasionally; and I don't see her stopping any time soon.

Mom occasionally, and understandably, gets a little frustrated or down when friends of hers become ill and pass away. It's a fact of life we'll all have to deal with at some point, but Mom takes care of herself and plans to be around quite a bit longer. One of my favorite sayings is something she said last winter. One of her best friends, whose husband is in a nursing home, innocently stated that she 'guessed their traveling days were over.' As Mom tells it, she went home and went to bed, then woke up and said, 'I'll be damned if I'm going to sit in my rocking chair and watch the world go by.' Right after that, Mom joined a travel club and surrounded herself with fun, positive, adventurous people. She's one of the oldest in the group and is considered by many to be their surrogate grandmother. She just returned from a trip to the Dominican Republic, enjoying the beach with my family. And I'm looking forward to seeing what paintings she tackles next! When asked what her plans are, she 'just wants to keep getting better.' And her advice to anyone *who wants to be an artist: 'Get started! You do have to work at it; but you'll never know until you try!'*

At a time in life when many people think they're too old to start again, she chose to see the possibilities and pursued her dreams. I can only hope that I'm as active, positive, strong, and creative when I reach her age! I'll consider that a very worthwhile, fulfilling life!"

If you'd like to comment or share your own story with Mary Ann or Janette, please visit *www.ThePathThatBeckons.com.*

Chapter 12

The Path of Inner Bliss

*"To experience peace does not mean that your
life is always blissful. It means that you are
capable of tapping into a blissful state of mind
amidst the normal chaos of a hectic life."*
– Jill Bolte Taylor

Recently I was in Texas staying with my mother-in-law as she recovered from an injury. Even though she was a cooperative patient and an entertaining story-teller, the days were filled with household chores, visits from nurses and physical therapists, and trips to the doctors, which left me little time to myself. One morning I awoke early, poured myself a steaming hot cup of coffee, and stepped onto the back patio for a few minutes of relaxing quiet time before the day began. It was a cool, crisp morning. I was keenly aware of the moisture in the air and the lush green foliage which are both a direct contrast to the cacti, succulents, and dry air back home in Arizona. Her small yard is encircled with large oak trees and the ground is covered with unfamiliar (to me, at least) vines and flowers. I was serenaded by birds welcoming the new day as I sat there enjoying the first sips of my coffee. The only thing missing from this idyllic moment in time would have been for a delicate butterfly to gracefully light on my hand.

All of a sudden, I became aware of a sound I hadn't heard before. It was the noise of traffic, lots of it. Her house is relatively near the interstate, although there are plenty of barriers between the two: a fence, a side road, a grouping of trees, another road, a section of businesses, a frontage road, and then the freeway. Even with all those blockages, the sound of vehicles driving by became deafening to me. How could it be that just seconds earlier I hadn't heard it, but now I couldn't NOT hear it? My peaceful energy and focus shifted to the distraction of the noise. My mood made a U-turn (get it?) from joy and serenity to discomfort and irritation. I reluctantly picked up my coffee cup and went inside to finish my morning drink in silence.

Has this ever happened to you? One minute you're in this blissful place, and then a tiny distraction or annoyance appears and BAM! your peacefulness is gone?

I relied on outside sights and sounds to determine my happiness that morning; and when something I didn't consider conducive appeared, my joy was gone. How often do you do this? Do you get up in the morning waiting for something to determine the tone for your day? If the first thing you discover is breakfast waiting for you, do you decide the day is going to be a good one? But then your car won't start. Does it now become a bad day? Our default in living life many times is simply reacting to our conditions and letting them gauge our mood, and, quite literally, our joy.

What if we realized our joy lies within, and regardless of what's going on "out there" we have access to a wellspring of inner bliss? It's true. It's not always easy. But it's true.

It's a bit like meditation. When I began meditating, I couldn't stay focused for longer than five seconds. Then, what is commonly called the monkey-mind would come in and wreak havoc. I would make shopping lists in my head, replay my chores for the day, recall songs I hadn't thought of in years, and I won't even go into the random nonsense that appeared in my brain. The point is it's not easy to be still. As I persisted, I developed a practice, and as my distracting thoughts began to ease in and overtake the silence, to myself I whispered, "Shh." Then in about ten seconds, again, "Shh." The intervals between the chatter-fest got longer and longer until I could remain in that stillness for extended periods of time. By no stretch of the imagination have I mastered meditation (if that's even possible). There are many days I give in to the monkey-mind and forego the process, just so I can jot down that unceasing list that's screaming to be acknowledged. This is a practice which requires conscious and consistent effort to improve, and it doesn't always go as we'd like it. The same is true with connecting to the peace within. It's not easy at first, and helps to rely on outside methods to reach that place. With practice, we get better at finding our peace, and, as a result, can maintain a connection to that peace for longer periods of time regardless of what's going on in the world around us.

Let's explore ways of connecting with our inner bliss. I imagine this practice in stages, and as each is mastered you naturally evolve into the next phase.

Phase One calls on outside stimuli to access your inner bliss. I have a friend who practices what she calls a "joy ritual." For her, it's a small action that takes her directly to her joy and lights her up. What is yours? You may say, "I don't have one," but I dare say you do. You just may not recognize it. Maybe it's holding that sweet child or grandchild and feeling their soft face and warm breath against your neck. Maybe it's tossing a ball to your dog and experiencing his happy face and wagging tail as he playfully returns it to you. It could be looking through a photo album and reminiscing over pleasant memories, dancing around the house to music you love, or singing at the top of your lungs as your drive with the windows down in your car on a country road. How about savoring your favorite cup of tea while snuggled with a fluffy blanket reading a captivating book? It could be something as simple as putting a drop of your favorite essential oil on your wrist to smell occasionally, or treating yourself to a decadent piece of dark chocolate.

Triggers can instantly transport you to that state of inner bliss. Recognize and appreciate them. Don't hesitate to tap into them as often as possible. Notice what brings you instant serenity. Once there, focus on maintaining the feeling, not allowing outside distractions to rob your joy. Remember, you have control over your reaction to all things.

As your "joy ritual" becomes a natural part of your daily life, you may see yourself moving into Phase Two. In this phase, instead of using triggers in life to feel at peace, your awareness is heightened and you begin experiencing bliss from unexpected sources. Sights, sounds, and aromas you hadn't noticed before will grab your attention. Walking to the mailbox, you may notice the smell of blossoms on a rose bush, even though you've passed that place hundreds of times oblivious to its sweet scent. The sunset may appear unusually breathtaking and you'll wonder why you've failed to notice it before as you drove home from work. The shift is that you're not looking for things to make you happy. You already are happy, and as a result you are conscious of the things that add to your happiness.

It's in this phase that you start to expect good things. The more connected to your inner joy you become, the more joy you recognize. The more joy you recognize, the more comes in. It's an age-old concept that what you think about and focus on expands. It's represented in many ways and in many beliefs: "As a man thinks, so he is;" the Law of Attraction; like attracts like; what comes around goes around; karma; and the list goes on and on.

Call it what you will, but notice as you become more centered and grounded in joy and love at your core. You can't help but see more and more to be joyful about.

This doesn't mean that your life will become perfect or that you won't have trials and pain. As long as you're living on this planet, you'll have those experiences. But now you have access to that inner reservoir that lifts you up and pulls you through those times. It's also a fun phase, because at several points during your day you'll find yourself recognizing how many times your spirit continues to be lifted and your well of joy refilled.

Phase Three, my personal favorite, is when you are no longer surprised by the little beauties coming your way each day. You still recognize them and express appreciation. They've become a natural part of your world. You expect them now, and you've gotten to the point where you're in a state of peace and joy more often than not instead of the other way around. You're adequately prepared to accept unwanted situations and hardships that come your way. You've learned how to go inward and pull strength and joy from that deep knowing that all is well.

It's in this phase where your focus begins to shift outward instead of inward. You are now in a place where you can help others. Instead of beginning your day waiting to see what will occur to facilitate a "good" or "bad" day, you ask yourself how you can help someone else have a better day. Is there a word of encouragement you can offer someone who's struggling? Can you initiate a phone call and put a smile on someone's face? Would it make your partner's day if you simply texted them "I love you"? As with meditation or all worthwhile disciplines, it takes practice, and with practice you'll notice it evolving into a natural way of being for you. The energy of love, joy, and peace you extend will come back to you a hundred-fold. As you share the bliss you've discovered with others, your heart will swell and your soul enlarge.

Most of the paths we've explored together in these pages offer an opportunity to turn our focus within, to heal what's asking to be healed, to accept what needs to be accepted, and to love ourselves right where we are. I believe it's absolutely crucial to heal our own hearts before we can fully support and love others. As they say, "You can't give what you don't have to give." Once you take positive, powerful steps toward healing, know you deserve to be happy. Believe it's truly possible. Everything works together for your good.

I hope if you take away anything from this book, you master this path. The greatest gift you can give yourself is tapping into that deep inner knowing where all your peace, love, and bliss reside. It's a place in your soul that will comfort you in your darkest hours, and encourage you when you feel like quitting. It will ground and center you; and you will know who you are at your core by living a life of passion, joy, and purpose.

This path will carry you home.

Today's Step

Make a list. (You know by now I love lists; and this is my last opportunity to ask you to do one. Sniff.) Keep this list with you throughout the day and jot down everything that adds to your happiness. Be careful not to use these things to MAKE you happy, because you're already going to be connected to your bliss, right? Don't be too hard on yourself. Have fun with it. Let yourself be amazed by all that's conspiring to add to your joy! Oh, yeah, and don't forget to be grateful.

Mayra's Story (names have been changed)

I was privileged to meet an incredible woman named Mayra, who took the idea of the Path of Inner Bliss quite literally. She was living in Florida and working as a pre-school teacher. It was a decent job. She loved the children; but the work situation wasn't ideal. She found herself wondering if this was all there was to life.

She was very close to her aunt, Tante Kathe, a tough yet tender woman who emigrated from Germany and was like a mother to her, especially since her own mother had passed away. They shared a special bond only nieces and aunts understand. When she was told the heartbreaking news that her aunt was diagnosed with cancer, Mayra was understandably shaken and deeply saddened. The prognosis was 6-8 months. Even though Mayra was told she had a little time, she felt an urgency to visit her dear tante immediately.

The two women shared a most memorable time together as they talked about everything from recipes to the meaning of life. Mayra's aunt asked her if she was happy, to which she quickly assured her she was. The wise matriarch wasn't completely satisfied with the answer, as she continued by stressing to Mayra that it was important for her to know that her sweet niece was truly happy. She lovingly urged her to do whatever it took to reignite her joy and made her promise she would.

That was the last conversation the two women shared. Her beloved Tante Kathe passed away the next day with Mayra at her bedside.

Their heartfelt conversation regarding real happiness lingered with Mayra. She couldn't get it out of her head, and was forced to admit to herself she could NOT say she was truly happy. But she didn't know what would make her happy. So she did something radical.

She quit her job and decided to use the money she had been saving for a rainy day to explore this elusive concept of "happiness." After all, she couldn't think of a rainier day than today.

She did her research, bought a backpack, hiking boots, tent, supplies and granola bars; and Mayra set out to walk. She wasn't exactly sure where she was going or how long it would take her. She just knew she needed a break, that her heart needed to heal, and she really wanted to be happy.

She embarked on her path of healing in Northern Georgia and began heading northeast along the Appalachian Trail. She hiked and she hiked. She hiked for a total of four months, ending up in Albany, New York!

Her long days of solitude were spent in self-reflection and deep soul searching of what she was called to do next. She discovered a spirituality and profound connection with her Creator that was very different from what she was taught in the church she attended as a child. She was amazed by that realization, as she didn't believe it even existed within her. She reflected on her life and all the really good things that were part of it. She also acknowledged the "not so great" parts and received answers to many situations she'd been struggling with for some time. She discovered a courage and self-sufficiency in herself as she camped most nights just back off the trail of the path she was traveling.

Mayra found something amazing on this path. Mayra found Mayra. She became clear on what she wanted in life and how to go about it. She finished with a deep knowing that whatever her next pursuit entailed, she had the tools and ability to be happy. Her happiness didn't depend on the situation or the job. She discovered a precious gem by knowing that happiness and her own inner bliss are choices. And she could choose – again and again!

Afterword

E arlier this year, I had a literal path beckon to me, and I've called upon that experience a few times in the pages of this book. It was to walk the Camino de Santiago, the 500 mile pilgrimage in Spain. It proved to be unexplainable, life-changing, and profound. The pictures at the beginning of each chapter were taken with the camera on my cell phone at different points along the trail. I include those, and some of my reflections, as a way of bringing you with me on that journey.

The stories included in each chapter are my own experiences or that of real people in my life. I choose not to relate tales of famous people, past or present, because there are so many in my immediate circle of friends and acquaintances who are living amazing lives that I prefer to share those with you instead. My hope is that you to peer into your own world, recognizing the strength and inspiration of those you know as well. Allow these people to lift you up when times are tough and remind you that you're stronger than you think.

The paths we've explored are just the beginning. There are also paths of Authenticity, Finding Your Voice, Listening, Service, and the list goes on and on. I hope you sit with and discover for yourself what unique path is calling you right now, and venture out by taking steps in that direction, even if they're just baby steps at first.

My sincere desire is that you find at least one idea in these pages that sparks something within your heart and soul to light you up to the idea of living an authentic, fulfilling, and joy-filled experience to set you in motion. Be gentle with yourself. We're all navigating our way on this adventure called life doing the best we can. Move past whatever's holding you back from the past, be fully present and engaged where you are now, and open to the myriad of paths that beckon you into the ridiculously amazing life you deserve!

While walking the trail in Spain, I ran across these words written by a fellow pilgrim on a rock that I leave with you now:

I've walked this path you're walking now.
Even though we haven't met,
I know you.
I've experienced your joys.
I've felt your pain.
We are the same.

Much love on your journey, my fellow traveler,

Debbie

About the Cover and Its Creator

Ihad an idea for the cover of this book, but when I laid eyes on a mesmerizing photograph on the wall in my friend's healing arts studio, my mind was changed. I instantly fell in love with the photo and knew it was destined to take its rightful place on the cover of this book, inviting and welcoming seekers to explore *The Path that Beckons*.

I researched the photographer to ask permission to use this breathtaking work of art. In the first picture I saw of him, the photographer had a huge rugged beard and wore a bandana tied around his head. I have to admit, I was intimidated. He looked more like a tough biker than the sensitive artist stereotype I had in my mind's eye, but I would be proven wrong. Skip Nall, who I imagine in person to be like a big teddy bear (we have only communicated via email), allowed me to license his beautiful photograph. He was kind, supportive, and encouraging, especially when I revealed this was my first attempt at writing. His generous spirit is much appreciated; and I consider him an integral part of this labor of love.

Thank you, Skip.

Turns out the photograph and the bridge have an interesting story, which Skip shared with me and has given me permission to pass on to you.

"I had gone to Vietnam to photograph the country and people, and eventually made my way to Sapa. The trip there is a fun one in a way. We took an overnight train in a sleeper car and arrived at the station about 6:00 a.m.

I had arranged for a guide. After meeting with him I began the hike into the mountains to where I was to spend my first night with a native Hmong Indian family. My wife at the time was going to meet us nearby where the annual Tet Holiday was being celebrated along with the blessing of the rice terraces.

I saw the bridge and thought it had to be photo-graphed. It was new and was in pristine condition. What I found out later is that the bridge is not there so much for transportation, but for luck. There is a concrete bridge a stone throw away for bikes, cars, etc. This bridge is thought to bring luck to those who cross it. And from what I understand, you only cross the bridge going in the direction of the big tree on the other side."

I had my wife cross the bridge so that I could photograph a "hiker" on it. We had been trying to get pregnant and honestly had given up. A few months later she was pregnant with the daughter, who I am now a single father to, Jade, who is the joy of my life."

Please check out Skip's other works at *www.skipnallphoto.com.*

Jade Nall and her father, Skip.

About the Author

D ebbie loves encouraging, inspiring, and challenging people, especially women, to live their best lives! Everything she does comes from that belief. Whether she's at home in Scottsdale, Arizona, hosting a group of women for coffee, cake, and conversation, or in Ireland leading an inspirational retreat focused on gratitude, Debbie's passion is helping her fellow women achieve the dreams and visions they hold for their lives.

Her husband, Mike, has gotten used to her popping in and out of town balancing her time between empowering her many "sisters" and snuggling with him on the sofa. He lovingly encourages her to do what fills her soul.

As much as Debbie appreciates the privilege of being included in so many women's lives and thrives on sisterhood, her respite is her home. She treasures times shared with her children and grandchildren. With her entire family living in the Phoenix area, birthday celebrations in her home, along with special meals, decorations and cake, are numerous and a big deal!

In her quiet time, she enjoys reading, writing, and daydreaming in her comfy chair while soaking in the nature of her beautifully groomed and peaceful backyard, which is her husband's pride and joy.

She knows she is loved, and hopes to be a channel for that same love to flow through her. Her belief is that life is a precious gift not to be taken for granted. She strives to remember to live each day fully with a joyful heart of appreciation.

To check Debbie's schedule of events, please visit *www.DebbieLambTurner.com* or *www.ThePathThatBeckons.com.*

As connect with her on:

Twitter-@DebLambTurner

Instagram-DebbieLambTurner

Facebook-www.fb.com/DebbieLambTurnerAuthor

The Next Step

Thank you so much for taking time out of your hectic schedule to read *The Path That Beckons*. I do hope you gained many insights and experienced a few "Aha!" moments of clarity.

The material covered in the previous chapters is meant to serve as a starting place to venture down a new path – one that leads you to a life brimming with vitality and possibilities.

If you would like to delve more deeply into the topics in this book, or any other obstacles you may be facing, please visit *www.DebbieLambTurner.com* for information on upcoming workshops and retreats that provide extensive exploration with other like-minded women.

I also invite you to check back to my website often to receive helpful tools, such as devotionals, journals, and other items which are added on a regular basis.

30877370R10104

Made in the USA
San Bernardino, CA
25 February 2016